KILLER CULTS

JAMES J. BOYLE

St. Martin's Paperbacks

KILLER CULTS

ISBN: 0-312-95285-6

Printed in the United States of America

St. Martin's Paperbacks edition/ May 1995

10 9 8 7 6 5 4 3 2

Listlessly, the queue of the doomed filed along the table, hands mechanically dipping cups into vats of death. From the gathering darkness, hellish screams rose in crescendo. Most went blindly to their deaths, some of them shouting praise to their leader as they died, some hugging each other and saying calm good-byes before they drank. His voice hoarse, his mouth dry, his clothing soaked with amphetamine sweat, Jim Jones raved in the spotlight as the hollow faces of the dying faded from the light. "To me, death is not a fearful thing . . ."

Dear Reader:

The book you are about to read is the latest bestseller from St. Martin's True Crime Library, the imprint *The New York Times* calls "the leader in true crime!" Each month, we offer you a fascinating account of the latest, most sensational crime that has captured the national attention. St. Martin's is the publisher of perennial bestselling true crime author Jack Olsen (SON and DOC) whose SALT OF THE EARTH is the true story of how one woman fought and triumphed over life-shattering violence; Joseph Wambaugh called it "powerful and absorbing." DEATH OF A LITTLE PRINCESS recounts the investigation into the horrifying murder of child beauty queen JonBenét Ramsey; the author is Carlton Smith. Fannie Weinstein and Melinda Wilson tell the story of a beautiful honors student who was lured into the dark world of sex for hire in THE COED CALL GIRL MURDER.

St. Martin's True Crime Library gives you the stories *behind* the headlines. Our authors take you right to the scene of the crime and into the minds of the most notorious murderers to show you what really makes them tick. St. Martin's True Crime Library paperbacks are better than the most terrifying thriller, because it's all true! The next time you want a crackling good read, make sure it's got the St. Martin's True Crime Library logo on the spine—you'll be up all night!

Charles E. Spicer, Jr.
Senior Editor, St. Martin's True Crime Library

Table of Contents

Introduction

FIRST, A WORD about the devil.

For well over a decade the media have been spreading shocking accounts that, taken together, would seem to indicate that a vast, secret network of fanatical cultists have been preying on decent society, committing unspeakable acts of ritual murder, child abuse, human mutilation, cannibalism, and other heinous crimes in the name of Satan.

These lurid tales are myths—partly created, like the giant alligators of the New York City sewers—through an excess of credulity and a lack of common sense. The human need to find focus for fear and apprehension is a powerful one. The devil one can't see is, perhaps, more terrifying than the devil one can see.

I refer anyone interested in the subject of satanic cults to two books published in 1993: *Remembering Satan: A Case of Recovered Memory and the Shattering of an American Family,* by Lawrence Wright, which originally appeared as a series in the *New*

Yorker; and *Satanic Panic: The Creation of a Contemporary Legend,* by Jeffrey S. Victor.

This book—except for those instances when Satan takes his bows among the cast of characters parading through the deranged mind of a psychopath like Adolfo de Jesus Constanzo—is not about the devil, but about an evil that can be seen, documented, and learned from: the twenty-five-year span of dangerous cults that began with the Manson Family and most recently blazed into the headlines on the plains near Waco, Texas. Such cults are assembled by charismatic figures like David Koresh—epic megalomaniacs who have no interest in associating themselves with Satan, who is, after all, folklore's single biggest loser (even Manson redefined his devil in service to a vengeful God).

Real killer cults nearly always claim to be on the side of the righteous. Some actively prey on the world outside their tightly controlled borders. Others —like Koresh's Branch Davidians or Philadelphia's Move—insist that they left other people alone, and all they ever wanted was to be left alone in return. When their illegal actions or apocalyptic street theater goad the police into ill-advised violent confrontations, their supporters blame only the police. I hope these stories show that they cannot in good conscience justify that.

As the millennium approaches with the start of the next century, hysteria and fanaticism about the end of the world—one of the favorite themes of killer cults—will accelerate. From Manson to Jones to Koresh, the dangers posed by destructive cults have been clear and persistent for a quarter century. Whether the authorities, the news media, and the public have learned from them is something that remains to be seen.

CHAPTER ONE

❧ ❧ ❧

Summer of Love

His BIRTH CERTIFICATE identified him merely as "No Name Maddox," but by the time he was through, there wouldn't be any problem remembering the name.

By the late summer of 1969, the horrors had already been going on for some time, quietly. But they burst into the headlines on a sultry Saturday morning, August 9, from the sun-dappled seclusion of an estate on a road that ambles for a short distance in Bel Air, high on the mountain where Benedict Canyon plunges down to Beverly Hills.

Winifred Chapman, a maid, first noticed something amiss when she arrived for work at 10050 Cielo Drive around eight A.M. A telephone wire, sliced with a knife, dangled uselessly over the steel-mesh front gate. Since whoever cut it had obviously made no attempt to conceal the fact, she did not give too much thought to the matter, assuming it to be an unfinished job by a phone company worker. She picked up the morning paper from the ground and let herself in.

But on the well-manicured lawn just inside the gate, she noticed another odd sight: an old white Rambler sedan parked haphazardly just off the winding drive, its front tires turned sharply into the matted wet grass. The cars here usually were foreign and expensive—sleek Mercedes or Ferraris, not boxy Ramblers. Picking up her pace, Mrs. Chapman made her way inside the house to the kitchen, where she typically started her workday before the residents—movie people—arose late in the morning. The house was very quiet, which was normal enough for the hour. She held the phone to her ear to check for a dial tone. It was dead.

That was when she saw the blood, a small glistening pool of it on the rich Italian tiles of the kitchen floor. Frowning, the maid saw that a faint trail of blood led through the dining room along the living room floor. Following it, she nearly stumbled on two blood-soaked bathroom towels wadded up on the rug beside a couch.

Off to the right she could see sunlight knifing in through the half-open door to the garden. The maid hurried over to close it, but she stopped short. Finally, she screamed. Across the door, someone had scrawled the word PIG. The epithet was written in blood.

Outside, on the gentle slope of the lawn just beyond the border of three-foot hedges, she found the first two bodies—a white male in his early thirties, his bell-bottom jeans, purple shirt, and low-cut boots stained in blood, his flesh ragged with slash wounds, his skull bashed in. Beside him, in a bloody full-length white nightgown, sprawled a dark-haired woman in her mid-twenties. Her limbs also were severely slashed.

There was no escaping the carnage. Running hysterically back into the living room, the maid found a pretty blond woman, the mistress of the house, more than eight months pregnant, lying in a fetal position, clad only in bra and panties. Her body, sprawled in front of the fireplace, was slashed from head to thigh. Around her slim neck was a loop of rope, which had been tossed over a wood ceiling beam and then fastened around the neck of the other body on the floor, a male in a blue shirt and white trousers, also slashed.

There was one more. Inside the Rambler, slumped dead on the front seat, was an eighteen-year-old boy, the only one of the bodies that the maid did not recognize.

She ran screaming from the property. Down the street, she finally saw another person, a fifteen-year-old boy.

"There's bodies and blood all over the place!" she cried. "Call the police!"

The headline in the next morning's newspaper terrified those who had awakened with a shudder to the bloodcurdling screams echoing blindly in the night over the hills of Benedict Canyon: RITUAL MURDERS!

Charles Manson and his Family, leering from the headlines like demons, had announced the start of a new American nightmare.

Charles Milles Manson didn't really fit the profile of a cold-blooded mass murderer. At first glance he seemed more like what he had started out as in his criminal life: a small-time car thief with a chip on his shoulder—a dim-witted punk who robbed gas stations for spending money. He was more the hair-triggered hoodlum who might shoot a gas station attendant in a panic, and then run and hide. Physically cowardly, shifty-eyed, loudmouthed, surly, desperate for attention—he didn't really appear to have the volition, patience, or boldness to commit premeditated mass murder, let alone actually persuade others to kill in his name. Only a unique intersection of man and era could create the specter of Charlie Manson, whose evil grin would become a hobgoblin for the sixties, leering toward the millennium.

Charlie was born in Cincinnati in 1934 to an unmarried teenage girl named Kathleen Maddox. Asked to provide a name for the infant's birth certificate, the mother had been stumped. Thus he entered society as "No Name Maddox." It wasn't until a few months later that the boy became Charles, and a few years after that came the surname Manson, after a man his mother briefly married.

When Charlie was not quite five, his mother was sent to prison for robbing a gas station, and he was taken in by an intensely religious aunt and uncle in West Virginia. But the young Charlie apparently did not get religion, at least not the way his foster parents envisioned it.

By the age of twelve he was in an Indiana reform school. That was where the first official notation of young Charlie's budding personality was entered. When he wanted to be, he could be a "likable boy," the institution's records said. But (and perhaps understandably) the boy was already showing signs of a "persecution complex."

Charlie soon escaped from reform school and managed to locate his mother, who was out on parole. She told him to get lost, and he did. In the process, he held up stores and was caught red-handed during a nighttime burglary.

Thanks partly to the ability he had to turn on a degree of manipulative charm when it suited him, Charlie managed to get himself sent to Father Flanagan's Boys Town, the charitable home in Nebraska. There, he sorely taxed the institution's famous slogan that "There is no such thing as a bad boy." He lasted all of four days, before stealing a car and committing two armed robberies.

A repeat offender by thirteen, in and out of penal institutions over the next few years, Charlie committed his first federal felony at the age of sixteen when he and two other boys escaped from a reformatory and crossed state lines on a crime spree to California, robbing gas stations in stolen cars along the way. Caught red-handed again, Charlie graduated to a federal juvenile center.

Prison psychiatrists were intrigued by the stubbornly illiterate young man. He was evaluated as unstable, antisocial, but "criminally sophisticated"—a diagnosis that seemed questionable since he was always caught so readily. Criminal aptitude aside, Charlie did exhibit enough jailhouse social skills to instinctively understand how to say what people wanted to hear. After a period of psychotherapy—which he submitted to eagerly, since he loved attention—he impressed his therapists as stable and level-headed enough to be considered rehabilitated and ready for freedom. A parole hearing was scheduled.

As usual, Charlie ran into trouble. A month before

the hearing, he brutally sodomized another boy at knifepoint. Instead of being paroled, he was shipped to a tougher federal reformatory.

The cycle repeated itself. Back behind bars, he learned to impress his guards with cunning and cordiality; he even took some classes to try to learn how to read, though without great success. In 1954, nineteen years old, he was paroled. Free again, Charlie met and married a seventeen-year-old waitress. Though they had a son together, he had little time for fatherhood. Instead, he concentrated on stealing cars, a pursuit for which he had shown little talent in the past. Of course, he was caught.

Once again in prison, this time in California, the hapless con fell under two influences that would prove to be crucial in his later life. One, seemingly innocuous, was modern psychological "motivational" training, in which the social and business networking principles of such popular self-improvement help gurus as Dale Carnegie were combined with intense group therapy and so-called "mind dynamics" sessions. Charlie naturally excelled at this.

The other was a more traditional form of jailhouse education. He attached himself to an older inmate, who had been associated with the Ma Barker gang and who taught Charlie, among other less useful things, how to play the guitar.

A star was born, if only in his own mind. In March of 1967, released on parole, having spent more than half of his life in the rigidly structured world of prison, with his beat-up guitar and thirty-five dollars in his pocket, Charlie took a bus for San Francisco and turned himself into a hippie rock musician, just in time for the fabled Summer of Love.

To a self-absorbed ex-con with no skills other than the ability to manipulate people and mimic records, San Francisco in the summer of 1967 was a paradise of free-flowing drugs, willing women, and unchecked hedonism, all coated with a thin veneer of idealism. Charlie worked the scene like a burglar. As an older man with outlaw mystique, which he skillfully combined with a cultivated hippie image, Charlie didn't have to panhandle the streets with his guitar for long before he scored. He struck up a conversation with a shy, homely, twenty-three-year-old assistant librarian named Mary Brunner, moved into her apartment, and settled into life in the teeming Haight.

Charlie quickly disabused Mary of any notions she had about monogamy. He brought home another, much prettier young redhead, Lynette Fromme, whom he had picked up on a trip to Venice Beach, near Los Angeles, with this line: "I am the god of fuck." Fromme, a nineteen-year-old who had grown up in middle-class comfort in Santa Monica before dropping out, was nicknamed Squeaky because of her disconcerting high-pitched giggle. Though Mary resisted having Squeaky move in, Charlie easily prevailed. And once Squeaky was installed, other girls—most of them runaways recruited from the streets—began arriving. The allure was part crash pad, part Charlie himself, and, of course, the Haight itself.

Charlie's deliberately crafted image found a ready audience in the Haight, where hallucinogenic chemicals smoothed over rough emotional edges while acid-rock music pumped redemption into bare souls. With people constantly drifting in and out of the Manson household, the core group soon numbered more than a dozen—including a few young men, brought home by the girls and the promise of sex, drugs, and rock and roll. They called themselves the Family. From the beginning, Charlie sat at the head of the table.

Arrayed around him were the desperate by-products of a culture that offered but two alternatives: stardom or despair. Charlie "gave off a lot of magic," the stolidly loyal Squeaky Fromme later enthused. "He was a changeling. He seemed to change every time I saw him." Dreamily, she recalled that Summer of Love: "We were riding on the wind."

The wind was actually howling in from hell, but the merry blaze of drugs, music, and companionship of the mutually disenfranchised offered a haven. Charlie presided over all activities in the household, where Family members found comfort thinking of themselves as gentle, idealistic "flower people"—a pose that was ludicrous in light of Charlie's incessant ramblings about killing "niggers." As such, the Manson Family was perfectly emblematic of the Haight of the late sixties, long after the comparatively innocent LSD-spiked milieu of a few years earlier, when the Jefferson Airplane and the Grateful Dead were neighborhood bar bands and Ken Kesey and his Merry Pranksters were on the loose. As the sixties waned, the ruthless drug trade, as much as drugs themselves, dominated Haight life. The flowers were props placed on streets thick with cynical opportunism.

In his book *The Family,* Ed Sanders described the "frenzy" that had engulfed the once-gentle Haight-Ashbury district by the summer of 1967, as the marketing engines of the music industry relentlessly hyped the hippie experience. "The word was out all over America to come to San Francisco for love and flowers," Sanders wrote. Like jackals to a watering hole, criminal opportunists flocked to such a scene. Besides runaways and would-be hippies fleeing suburban stultification, "the Haight attracted vicious criminals who grew long hair. Bikers tried to take over the LSD market with crude, sadistic tactics. Bad dope was sold by acne-faced methadrine punks . . . People began getting ripped off in the parks. There was racial trouble."

Charlie, with his remarkable ability at winning friends and influencing people, positioned himself to take full advantage of the opportunities. Though well into his thirties, Charlie perfected a role as sensitive hippie, even carefully grooming his own hair and beard to resemble popular conceptions of Jesus Christ. As he worked on his "music," Charlie proclaimed that he was going to become "bigger than the Beatles." Meanwhile, as he drew his followers ever closer together in a constricting world of isolation and paranoia, he began introducing fanatical religious elements into the spiritual mix.

Though still barely literate, he had managed to acquaint himself in prison with the favorite Scripture of paranoids, the Book of Revelation—the book of the Bible that most resembles an acid-rock album cover, with its evocations of multiheaded horned beasts, mystical signs in the heavens, and apocalyptic cataclysms in which the righteous slaughter the damned in a blaze of glory. Amply dosed with LSD, brimming with the maniacal metaphors of Revelation, Charlie announced that he had experienced his own epiphany in the Haight: Armageddon was at hand! And he, the former No Name Maddox, would be the one to brandish the terrible sword and lead the faithful to salvation.

While undergoing this theological awakening, Charlie had fallen in briefly with some Scientologists, members of a cult with which he had had some contact in prison. For a time, he tried to mimic their abstruse rhetoric, but without commitment. More to his liking was another influential Haight-based cult called the Process, a bizarre group of satanists that had been founded in England by a renegade Scientologist named Robert Moore. From their run-down house on Cole Street, two blocks away from the place where Manson and his Family lived, the black-caped Process preached a lifestyle that combined the depraved melodrama of satanic ritual with the usual measures of hallucinogenic drugs—laced together with talk of violence.

The Process was good at self-dramatization, Nazi imagery, and depiction of necrophilia. But membership required blind allegiance to a leader believed by the group to be Christ. Fresh out of prison, unwilling to take orders from anyone, secretly terrified of any male whom he could not readily dominate, Manson quickly lost interest in the Process.

But bringing his notoriously short attention span into full focus, he did borrow various Process theories that appealed to him. Chief among them was the notion that Christ and Satan had united in a divine alliance as the end of the world approached. Satan's job in Armageddon would be to slay the damned as a favor to Christ, Charlie decided. To a mind capable of putting that notion together, it was not a great leap to volunteer for the job himself. Charlie, then, was the avenger. Impatient for his Armageddon, he started openly advocating group violence as a way to bring about the Final Days. As a lifelong racist like Charlie figured it, white America—incensed by crimes committed by radical groups such as the Black Panthers—would go to battle against black America, resulting in nuclear war. When the dust settled, Charlie and his followers would emerge from a hiding place in the desert and take command of the resulting New Order. To bring all of this about would require igniting the racial war, and Charlie claimed the way to start it was to blame blacks for a wave of shocking violent incidents.

Laying such grand plans within the parochial confines of San Francisco was difficult, however. The Haight, teeming with newly minted hippies, was also jammed with tour buses. Rattling with the jackhammers of gentrification, the Haight was rapidly losing its allure for the communal satanic lifestyle dedicated to bringing about the end of the world.

The Process helpfully blazed the trail. In 1968, led by a phalanx of bikers in full-dress regalia, a caravan of black-robed Process members wound down the coastal highway to Los Angeles. There, they resettled in a big house near the Sunset Strip, a neighborhood just beginning its degeneration into a postmodern landscape where tourists framed out faded images of moviedom in their cameras while ignoring the prostitutes, drug dealers, hustlers, beggars, con men, and wasted proselytizers grimly staking their claims to the forsaken precincts of Hollywood.

Shortly after the exodus of the Process, Manson and a dozen or so of his starstruck adherents followed the devil worshipers to Hollywood. There, the diminutive hippie Messiah quickly reestablished a lively commune. The Family was funded by drug-dealing, panhandling, and credit-card theft, and well-nurtured by a recruiting system in which young runaway girls, some of them barely into their teens, acted as sexual lures to attract new males. In this symbiotic Eden, Charlie craftily doled out the pleasures of sex and drugs, while manipulating the fragile group psyche to place himself as the source of authority and the facilitator not only of pleasure and security, but of intimidation, isolation—and growing, unfocused rage.

As with any bully, fear was the crucial weapon. Charlie quite consciously used it. "Getting the Fear," in fact, was the title of one of his standard motivational lectures. As people felt more afraid and alone in his presence, he fine-tuned the picture of himself as Jesus Christ, Superstar—as a man who would overcome betrayal and persecution to fulfill a destiny of greatness and eternal fame. One favorite ritual was to strap himself to a wooden cross in the Family house while other members stripped naked and engaged in group sex at his feet.

While sentimental hippie romanticism was celebrated in the Family's frequent sessions at which everyone would sing or play music, the group found no contradictions in Charlie's virulent racial bigotry, which he made little effort to conceal, and his insistence that the Family start stockpiling guns for its coming journey to the "wilderness" to wait out the end of the world. Charlie's social philosophy had now become fully defined along three sharp forks: the black race's sole purpose on earth was to be slaves to the white race; women existed solely for the sexual gratification of men; no human action is evil, especially not murder.

Hopelessly gullible, drug-addled followers like Susan Atkins found him irresistible. A twenty-one-year-old high school dropout who had worked as a topless dancer before wandering into the Manson fold, Susan told others that she firmly believed that Charlie literally embodied both Jesus Christ and Satan. Like Susan, other Manson followers were so desperate for a measure of emotional certainty that snippets of pop song lyrics could sound like the meaning of life, and a lifelong loser—an illiterate, bigoted, vile-tempered ex-con with a beard, long hair, and a persecution complex—could be seen to be like Jesus Christ.

"He is the king and I am his queen," gushed Susan, among the truest of the disciples. "Look at his name, Manson. *Man's son.* Now I have visible proof of God, proof the Church never gave me."

Sometime in 1968 Charlie obtained a beat-up Volkswagen bus, which was painted black and driven around southern California and into the desert on romps designed to evoke nostalgia for the fabled acid-and-love odyssey of Ken Kesey and his merry band. Charlie always brought his guitar, which he now played proficiently, performing mostly his own songs—songs that people in the music business would later describe as competent, but derivative, overwrought, and without artistic merit.

Yet Charlie was clever enough to make inroads into the periphery of the popular-recording industry. This was because he entered the picture at precisely the time when poseurs, con men, and marketing wizards were redefining the industry more as speed-demon spectacle than music. With little actual talent, but plenty of macho "attitude"—a posture of contempt and a carefully cultivated satanic sneer—Charlie usually managed to get an initial hearing. To some newly rich, young music executives, the pint-sized ex-con with the crazed eyes and the devoted cult offered an opportunity to flirt with what seemed like danger. None of them realized, until later, just how genuine that danger was.

One of the most important contacts Charlie made in Hollywood at this time was Dennis Wilson, the drummer for the Beach Boys. In the spring of 1968, Wilson had stopped to give a ride to a couple of female hitchhikers who turned out to be Manson Family members. They introduced him to Charlie. Before Wilson quite realized what was happening, Charlie and members of his hippie harem inserted themselves as frequent house guests at Wilson's palatial Sunset Strip residence, a place that had once belonged to Will Rogers. Simultaneously attracted and repelled, Wilson and his brother Brian, another Beach Boys member, even assisted Charlie in recording a demo record. What's more, Dennis introduced him to a television and music industry executive named Terry Melcher, who was the son of actress Doris Day. Melcher lived in Bel Air. The address was 10050 Cielo Drive.

A key convert to the Manson Family around the same time was Charles "Tex" Watson, twenty-three years old. Watson was typical of the young men who had now swollen the ranks of the Manson family to about forty. A tough talker, he was actually an insecure, self-absorbed mama's boy who had dropped out of college and overcome inertia just barely enough to drift to Los Angeles, where he had vaguely outlined aspirations of becoming a "star." He had been hitchhiking on the Strip when he was picked up by a driver who, to his astonishment, turned out to be Dennis Wilson. Wilson invited Tex to his house to "party." There, he met Charlie and some of his girls.

"Charlie pulled me toward him with his girls," Watson recalled later. "For the first time in my life I felt like somebody."

Later in the year, satisfied that his music career was on track, Charlie decided that the Family needed more room and a degree of seclusion to prepare for the next phase of his plan—the exodus to the wilderness to await the Final Days.

Family member Sandra Goode, the daughter of a wealthy stockbroker, told Charlie about a movie ranch out in the far reaches of the San Fernando Valley, thirty miles northwest of Los Angeles. Secluded in the hills, the sprawl of ramshackle buildings, including a dilapidated western-movie Main Street set, was formerly the home of silent-movie cowboy star William S. Hart. It was now owned by George Spahn, who sometimes rented it out to film companies for location work. Scouting the location, Squeaky Fromme prevailed on the blind, eighty-two-year-old Spahn to allow the Family to move into what were called the "outlaw" shacks on the rear of his property, in exchange for doing chores and tending the horses.

Close enough for an easy commute back into L.A., but backed up against the Santa Susanna Mountains in an area of the valley that was still largely uninhabited, the ranch was perfect for training and consolidating the Family. It was also located in a convenient geographical region near other secluded hideaways where much of the Los Angeles basin's drug warehousing and distribution operations were based.

After settling in, Family members fanned out on daily errands into the city and suburbs to panhandle and steal. They also developed special skills as night burglars who would sometimes choose a house at random and enter it while its inhabitants slept, on Charlie's orders. The cultists would creep about the premises, gleefully moving furniture without awakening the inhabitants. Charlie himself sometimes participated in this nocturnal activity, which he called "creepy-crawling." Later, some residents in and around Los Angeles would realize with a cold shudder that they had been visited in the dark by the Manson Family.

For its part, the Family would soon have to move again, Charlie declared, to the "wilderness"—a site he had chosen in Death Valley, where protection could be had from the "fallout" of nuclear war that Charlie said would result from the period of racial strife.

While they lingered at the ranch, the Family outwardly lived as a hippie commune, though the women seemed to do all of the chores. There was constant preparation for the Final Days. Weapons were stockpiled. Old Volkswagens were converted into "dune buggies," which roared up dirt roads loaded with naked cultists armed with machine guns.

Charlie preached hate while doling out the drugs and sex. By now the talk was frequently of murder. As Watson recalled, Charlie insisted that "there was no such thing as death, so it was not wrong to kill a fellow human being."

From the Beatles' 1968 *White Album*, Charlie had adapted a song called "Helter Skelter" as the Family's anthem. Though the title actually referred wistfully to an amusement park ride in England, Charlie claimed to have deduced in it a more ominous meaning. "Helter Skelter," he declared, referred to the end of the world—specifically to the activities that would ignite the race war that would bring the Family glory.

"It all made sense," said a Family member. With sufficient amounts of drugs and isolation, everything made sense.

Charlie was wily in maintaining his own control. When he distributed drugs like LSD, he always took a smaller dose than anyone else, Watkins would tell Vincent T. Bugliosi, the deputy L.A. District Attorney who prosecuted the Manson Family and later summarized the case in his book, *Helter Skelter*.

Isolation was crucial. Except for assigned missions to steal or creepy-crawl, "Charlie never wanted us to leave the ranch," Watson explained. But there were compelling reasons to stay, Watson said. "It was drugs, drugs, drugs . . . bags of acid and speed. The girls would go out and hitchhike and meet new guys and bring them to the ranch."

LSD and mescaline, pot and peyote, amphetamines, angel dust, heroin and cocaine, were available in abundance at the ranch, not only to the Family, but to the procession of drug-dealing bikers, gun freaks, and other outlaws who came and went. Charlie especially encouraged the girls to use sexual favors to lure members of outlaw motorcycle gangs, who he hoped to be able to call on in his anticipated war against what he had come to call the "pigs."

Not all of the visitors were criminals, however. To their later chagrin, legitimate music industry people like Melcher would be called on to explain their associations with the Manson gang. Melcher, for example, twice visited the Spahn ranch at Charlie's invitation, to hear him perform with some of the girls. Indeed, in the winter of 1969, Charlie himself drove down to Bel Air to drop in on Melcher at his Cielo Drive home, following what Charlie believed was Melcher's offer to help him record a song. But Melcher wasn't there. Rudely, Charlie was informed by someone in the house—perhaps a servant—that Melcher had moved. Charlie was furious at what he considered to be an insult. Secretly, he vowed he would return.

Back at the ranch, Charlie, who had taken to wearing a military sword on his belt, drew up a hit list of rich celebrities—"pigs" who were to be murdered in such a way that blame would be cast on black radicals. On his list were such names as Warren Beatty and Julie Christie. But at the top of that list was Terry Melcher.

The Family was now a weapon ready to be pointed, and Charlie decided that the time had come.

It is not known how many people Manson and members of his Family ultimately killed as part of Helter Skelter. Manson, though a chronic liar, once bragged that he had murdered thirty-five people by himself. It is known, however, how many the Manson Family killed in one blood-drenched month in the summer of 1969. From July 27 to August 26 of that year they slaughtered nine people.

The first one to die in that period was thirty-two-year-old Gary Hinman, who had made the fatal mistake of telling Charlie to go to hell. Hinman had been studying for his doctorate in sociology at UCLA, and living comfortably thanks to a lucrative sideline as a small-time mescaline manufacturer. This was the activity that brought him into routine contact with the Manson Family.

An adherent of a militant Japanese Buddhist cult, Hinman was both arrogant and short-tempered in his dealings with the Family. When a dispute arose with Charlie over money in a drug transaction—at the time when Charlie and the Family were working hard to put together enough cash to finance their exodus to Death Valley—Hinman unwisely thought he would stand his ground against Charlie's threats.

Late on the night of July 25, Charlie, his sword in hand, came to Hinman's house on Topanga Canyon Road to demand the money. When Hinman tried to throw Charlie out, threatening to expose him and his followers, Charlie sliced off his ear with the sword.

All night long Family members terrorized the bleeding Hinman, finally forcing him to sign papers transferring ownership of two of his vehicles, a minibus and a Fiat. But it wasn't enough. The next night, Charlie sent three followers back to Hinman's house: Bobby Beausoleil, a twenty-year-old aspiring rock musician with connections to Hollywood, Susan Atkins, and Mary Brunner.

Hinman was brutally stabbed to death. When they left, the Manson cultists fingerpainted the words

"Political Piggy" on a wall in their victim's blood, along with the crude drawing of a panther's claw—a ploy to lead police to suspect the Black Panthers in the murder.

Back at the ranch, the Family assembled for a late night music session. A new song was composed about the murder. Its refrain consisted of Hinman's dying words: "I wanted to live. I wanted to live."

The house on Cielo Drive, now sublet by friends of Terry Melcher, was next on Charlie's list for Helter Skelter. The tenants were a movie actress, Sharon Tate, twenty-six, and her husband, a thirty-four-year-old Polish director named Roman Polanski. They had been married a year before while working together on a movie called *The Fearless Vampire Killers.* Besides having a featured role in *Valley of the Dolls,* the soft-spoken, well-liked Tate had achieved a measure of celebrity by having appeared nude in *Playboy* magazine in photos taken by her husband.

In February the Polanskis had sublet the house on 10050 Cielo Drive, with its almost clichéd panoramic view of Los Angeles spread out far below. Polanski, still in Europe finishing work on a movie, planned to join his wife—now eight and a half months pregnant —about the middle of August.

On the night of August 9, Tex Watson later testified, Manson called him aside at the Spahn ranch, where an orgy had just concluded. Said Watson, "He was smiling. Total perfection. I would do anything he asked me to . . . He computed with me to go with three girls and kill people. He handed me a knife and a gun and told me to make it as totally gruesome and bloody as we could."

Selected to assist him were Susan Atkins, Patricia Krenwinkel, and Linda Kasabian. Linda, who had been at the ranch for only a month, was designated as the driver and lookout.

Charlie's orders left no room for confusion. "Go up to the house where Terry Melcher used to live," he told Watson. "Kill them, cut them up, hang them on the mirrors." Watson said that Manson evidently had only a vague idea of who was now residing at 10050 Cielo Drive. "He said something about movie stars living there," Watson recalled.

That night, Sharon Tate had three houseguests. One was Jay Sebring, a flashy thirty-five-year-old hairdresser who made a comfortable living as a stylist for male celebrities such as Robert Redford and Frank Sinatra. Tate and Sebring had once been engaged.

The other two guests were Abigail Folger, the flighty twenty-five-year-old heiress to the Folger coffee fortune, and her boyfriend, an unemployed Polish emigré whose name was Wojiciech "Voytek" Frykowski, thirty-two. On the night of August 9, as on many nights before, Frykowski and Folger had been using MDA, a hallucinogenic drug. Frykowski also was known as a dealer in LSD.

After parking the car on darkened Cielo Drive outside the residence sometime just past midnight, the intruders creepy-crawled onto the grounds. Carrying a cowboy-style .22 revolver and a forty-foot coil of nylon rope, Watson first shimmied up a telephone pole and sliced the telephone wires into the house. While Kasabian waited by the car, Watson, Atkins, and Krenwinkel—all carrying long knives—dropped over the fence onto the lush, moist grass.

As the intruders crouched in the long shadows of the circular driveway, a car drove up. At the wheel was an eighteen-year-old youth, Stephen Earl Parent, arriving for a late night visit to his friend, the young caretaker of the house, William Garretson, who lived in a guest cottage at the rear of the grounds. Seeing the furtive trio in his headlights, Parent stopped, rolled down his window, and asked them what they were doing.

In response, Watson stepped forward, leveling his gun through the window.

"Please don't hurt me," the young man cried, but Watson shot him in the head four times. Calmly, Watson reached across Parent's body and turned off the ignition. The shots had reverberated over the hills of Bel Air, but then all was quiet. There was no sign from the house that anything was amiss.

Watson stole up to the house and slit a screen in a window leading into a first-floor room that was being remodeled as a nursery. Smelling the fresh paint, he crept through the darkened first-floor rooms and let the others in through the front door. They snapped on the lights.

In the living room, Frykowski awoke to see Watson looming over him.

"What time is it?" Frykowski mumbled groggily.

"Be quiet," Watson growled. "Don't move or you're dead."

"Who are you and what are you doing here?"

The intruder replied simply, "I am the devil and I am here to do the devil's work. Now where is your money?"

But money wasn't really the reason they had come. They had really come to kill people whose names they did not even know, and they did so merely because Charlie told them to.

The slaughter was about to begin. Susan Atkins went upstairs to see who else was in the house. She looked into a bedroom and waved casually at Abigail Folger, who was reading in bed and just waved back. Walking down the hall, Susan found Tate and Sebring talking quietly on the bed in the master bedroom. Brandishing her knife, she ordered the three of them to follow her downstairs.

There, the horrified victims found Watson holding a gun on Frykowski. Watson ordered them all to lie on the floor on their stomachs in front of the fireplace.

"Can't you see she's pregnant?" Sebring shouted, lunging for the gun. Watson fired, the bullet entering through Sebring's armpit.

Again money was demanded. Folger fumbled with her purse. It contained seventy-two dollars.

Watson was too busy uncoiling the rope to take the money. He looped it around the neck of the wounded Sebring, and then around the necks of Tate and Folger beside him on the floor. As he did this, Susan struggled to bind the terrified Frykowski's hands with a towel from the bathroom.

Sebring kept resisting. Furiously, Watson began stabbing him into silence, then tossed the rope over a long ceiling beam and hoisted the dead man and the two women up with it. Tate and Folger had to stand on their toes to avoid being strangled.

"You are all going to die." Watson told them.

He ordered Susan to kill Frykowski. But Frykowski broke free and ran toward the front door. As he stumbled into the garden, he was stabbed repeatedly in the back. He lay writhing twenty feet from the front door. His screams were so loud that they carried through the night across the canyon.

Watson pulled the trigger, but when the gun jammed, he pummeled the man's head with the butt.

Hearing the screams from her position by the car, Kasabian was horrified. "Please make it stop!" she called out to Susan on the lawn.

It was far too late for that.

Back in the living room, the two female victims worked desperately to get free from the rope. Folger managed to run toward the garden, but Atkins was right behind, stabbing her repeatedly as they ran. As Folger slumped to the ground, Watkins joined in the orgiastic slashing until she was dead.

Returning to the living room, Watson told Atkins to stab Tate, who was pleading, "Please don't kill me! All I want to do is have my baby!"

"Look, bitch, I don't care about you," Atkins muttered coldly, looking the actress in the eye while raising her knife. "I don't care if you're going to have a baby. You better be ready. You are going to die." Accompanied by Watson and Krenwinkel, they slashed at the pregnant actress, stabbing her sixteen times.

Atkins later said she licked the blood off her own hand. "Wow, what a trip," she said. "I felt so elated. Tired, but at peace with myself. I knew this was just the beginning of Helter Skelter. Now the world would listen."

As she left the house, Atkins dipped the towel in

Sharon Tate's blood and lingered by the front door to dab the word PIG on it.

Outside, the killers changed clothes in their car, where Kasabian waited. They then drove aimlessly on the winding streets of Bel Air, stopping at a desolate embankment near Mulholland Drive at the crest of the mountain to hurl the knives and their bloody clothes over a cliff. Nearby, they parked the car outside a house and used a garden hose to wash the car. They fled when the owner came outside.

When they got back to the ranch at two A.M., Charlie was waiting, stark naked.

"What are you doing home so early?" he inquired casually.

Tex could barely control his excitement. "Boy, it sure was Helter Skelter!" he said.

The next day, Susan learned who she had killed while watching news bulletins on television. "My reaction was, 'Wow, they sure are beautiful people,' " she later said, adding that she had been thrilled to have been so close to a celebrity like Sharon Tate. "It really blew my mind."

The grisly killings threw Hollywood into a panic. Charlie was delighted. There was a dope party back at the ranch to celebrate. Plans were immediately made for a new raid to strike more horror into the hearts of the pigs. Charlie announced that he himself would lead this one, to show how it was done. And there was no time to waste, now that blood was flowing. It was set for the next night.

Charlie, Watson, Atkins, Krenwinkel, and Kasabian—along with Family members Steve Grogan and Leslie van Houten—drove around for a few hours.

In Pasadena they stopped outside one house, chosen at random. Charlie crept up to the windows, but came back and announced that the residents would be spared because he had seen photographs of children displayed in the living room.

With Charlie giving directions, they then drove down to the Los Feliz neighborhood near Griffith Park in Los Angeles. They parked outside a big house 3301 Waverly Drive, the residence of Leno LaBianca, the middle-aged owner of a chain of supermarkets, and his wife Rosemary.

Shortly after one A.M., Leno LaBianca was sitting in his living room reading the newspaper, which was filled with stories about the gruesome murders in Benedict Canyon. His wife was in the bedroom. LaBianca looked up and saw a short, grizzly-looking man standing silently in front of him, holding a gun. He was astonished that the intruder had managed to get in without a sound.

"Be calm," Charlie told him. "Be quiet. You won't be harmed." That was a lie.

He led LaBianca to the bedroom and tied him up beside his wife. Then he walked out to the car.

"Tex, Katie, Leslie, go into the house. I have the people tied up. They are very calm."

While Charlie remained outside, the Family grimly killed again. Rosemary LaBianca was kept on the bed with a pillowcase over her head. Her husband was led downstairs, where Tex Watson slashed his throat, leaving the serrated kitchen knife sticking in the victim's neck. Hearing her husband's screams, Rosemary LaBianca struggled upstairs. Van Houten —a petite, twenty-year-old former Campfire Girl who had sung in her church choir and played Sousaphone in her high school band—held down the woman so that Krenwinkel could stab her in the back. The slashing severed Rosemary LaBianca's spine.

In the living room, Leno LaBianca was writhing toward death. Watson rushed upstairs to gleefully join in the mutilation on the bed. In all, Rosemary LaBianca was stabbed forty-one times. Her husband was stabbed twelve times with a knife and fourteen times with a large meat fork. The word WAR was crudely carved into his belly. "Death to Pigs" and "Helter Skelter" were scrawled in the victims' blood on a refrigerator and a wall.

The murderers were thoughtful enough to feed the LaBiancas' three dogs, one of which licked blood off their hands. Then they all took showers in the LaBiancas' bathroom. They fixed themselves dinner. Grabbing some containers of chocolate milk from the refrigerator, they left.

At the ranch in the days afterward, Charlie stepped up preparations for the exodus to the desert. Things began moving rapidly, especially as the police started closing in—not on the killings but on drug dealing and theft in the region. But first there was the problem of Shorty Shea.

Donald Shea, a thirty-six-year-old ranch hand and horse trainer who had worked for Spahn for about fifteen years, had been getting on Charlie's nerves, and August 1969 was not a good time to get on Charlie's nerves. Shorty had previously incurred Charlie's wrath by marrying a black woman, and allowing her friends to visit the ranch. But Shorty sealed his doom when Charlie heard that the ranch hand had been trying to persuade the elderly Spahn to run the Family off.

On August 26, Charlie sentenced Shorty to death. He was promptly ambushed by members of the Family. "It was like carving up a Christmas turkey," Daniel Decarlo, a biker associated with the Family, later testified. (Decarlo was not present for the murder, but was told about it later by a Family member.) Shorty was cut into nine pieces, his arms and head lopped off.

Charlie's long run of luck began to falter a week later, when he was arrested, along with twenty members of the Family, during a police raid on the ranch in a car theft investigation. They were not yet suspects in the Hollywood murders, and all were released for lack of evidence. While the police had discovered the extent to which Manson controlled a dangerous cult, they did not manage to link the Manson Family to the sensational murders in Los Angeles until Susan Atkins began jabbering away behind bars. Atkins—in jail on an unrelated charge—blithely described to a cellmate the details of the murdering of Sharon Tate. The cellmate promptly informed a guard.

By the end of the year Charlie, along with Watson, Krenwinkel, Atkins, and Van Houten, had been charged with murder. All were ultimately convicted and sentenced to life imprisonment. Steve Grogan, a Spahn ranch hand, was also sentenced to life for decapitating Shorty. He would be released on parole fourteen years later. No charges were brought against Mary Brunner and Linda Kasabian, who testified for the prosecution. Several years later Charlie's loyal lieutenant Squeaky Fromme would receive a life sentence for a botched attempt to assassinate President Ford.

In 1970, on trial for murder, Charlie described himself in legal papers as "Charles Manson, also known as Jesus Christ, Prisoner." In court he took the opportunity to make a rambling hour-long lecture. To hear Charlie tell it, everybody but himself was to blame for the carnage.

"I never went to school," Charlie said, "so I never growed up to read and write too good, so I have stayed in jail and I have stayed stupid, and I have stayed a child while I have watched your world grow up. And then I look at the things that you do and I don't understand. You eat meat and you kill things that are better than you are, and then you say how bad, and even killers, your children are. You made your children what they are . . . These children that come at you with knives, they are your children."

CHAPTER TWO

🔥 🔥 🔥

Dad Knows Best

His MOTHER CALLED him Jimba and said he had the Holy Spirit in him.

"The boy will be a famous minister," she would enthuse, and the boast didn't seem to be idle. As a youngster growing up in rural Indiana during the Depression, little Jim Jones played preacher the way other boys played cops-and-robbers.

By the age of eight he could reel off long passages from his Bible. Though short-tempered with people, the dark-eyed youngster seemed to have a great love of animals. He often brought home stray cats and dogs. Only years later would it be remarked upon that the animals Jim adopted so often got sick and died suddenly under his care. The boy always buried them with elaborate "funerals," where he preached and sobbed at his loss.

His mother, Lynetta, made him a clerical robe to dress up in. By the time he was twelve the boy was a genuine neighborhood oddity—gathering crowds of youthful spectators with hellfire-and-brimstone sermons, even leading small groups of children to the creek, where he ceremoniously "baptized" them. He'd then head home, with the pennies and nickels they handed him jingling in his pockets.

His mother was right. The boy was a natural.

That was the most remarkable thing of all. Just as the children trailed after him to the creek, people always followed Jim Jones. His wife, Marceline, was one of the first.

They'd met and married when he was seventeen and starting a career as an apprentice Methodist minister in Indianapolis; Marceline was a pleasant but quiet twenty-one-year-old nurse. Soon after they were married, Marceline learned how restless her husband was when he fled the hierarchal constraints of Methodism for the more freewheeling opportunities of street preaching. In 1957, after raising cash selling South American monkeys door-to-door for twenty-nine dollars apiece, Jones hung a shingle, "People's Temple," outside a rented storefront in an Indianapolis neighborhood whose population was rapidly changing from white to black. Just like that, he had founded his own religion.

Hustling, the fast-talking preacher quickly managed to attract crowds of curiosity-seekers who came back week after week. As the church rolls grew, he and his wife began a family. In 1959 they had their own child, a son they christened Stephen Gandhi Jones, but they also adopted three minority orphan babies—two Asians and one black—to fill out what they called their "rainbow family." To those who had known the intensely religious young man as a teenager, this seemed somewhat unusual. Jim Jones had always been a bigot as a youngster. But he was foremost a wily opportunist, and a Bible-thumping white racist with "nigger" on his curled lips wasn't about to get ahead preaching to a congregation that was nearly all black. This was the late fifties; the airwaves resonated with the stirrings of civil rights and black social activism. Setting himself up as a religious activist with a calculated appeal to a transient black population in a big-city environment, Reverend Jones had found his niche. As always, he was in the right place at the right time to cash in.

He did this with gusto, using a bag of gimmicks and public relations tricks to build audience appeal, enhance his reputation, and bring in the donations. Posters attesting to his awesome abilities as a preacher, prophet, and faith healer fluttered from walls and telephone poles all over Indianapolis. While mainstream neighborhood churches dispensed their steady diet of hymns and homilies, Reverend Jones's People's Temple defined itself as an urban Christian mission—a place where people down on their luck and looking for comfort could find not only spiritual uplift, but also a meal, a bed, a sense of community in a rootless environment—and quite often, a job. Jones used the resulting pool of cheap labor to set up small businesses affiliated with—and channeling money into—the People's Temple.

Prosperity in turn attracted new and better-heeled followers, and soon the Temple was a thriving neighborhood institution that boasted a hundred-voice choir and attracted jubilant crowds to Sunday services. The Temple was a beehive of activity during the rest of the week too, as Jones expanded his base, leading his followers in fair-housing demonstrations and other New Left protests that generated respectful media attention and quickly established the charismatic young preacher as a new community leader. In 1961 he demonstrated his growing political clout when he was appointed director of the city Human Rights Commission.

With these successes came the flashy symbols of status—diamond rings, alligator shoes, frequent trips out of town in the style of a touring dignitary. By the early sixties Jones went everywhere surrounded by an entourage of aides and bodyguards. Some of his flock might well have remarked on the fact that Jones's top aides all were white—while the congregation was overwhelmingly black. If so, there is no record of it. From the beginning, Jones was alert for any sign of dissent. "Troublemakers" were isolated and dealt with at the first grumble of discontent.

While the Temple had begun to generate income from a number of outside sources, the "cash crop," as Jones called it, was always harvested from its growing membership. Along with the ever-circulating collection plates came frequent fund-raising drives in which congregants were expected to pledge wages or welfare and Social Security checks. Many went so far as to sign real estate and bank holdings directly over to Jones.

Jones was an effective preacher, but his forte was faith-healing. Like most faith-healers, he expertly orchestrated religious hysteria to provide cover for fraud and bunkum that utilized standard carnival tricks to deceive audiences. Impostors were hired to pose as cripples who would cast off their wheelchairs and crutches when "healed" by Jones. Spies working for Jones furtively compiled detailed notes on the quirks, confidences, and offhand comments of members of the congregation, who would then be flabbergasted to hear the preacher name them—and disclose their secrets—from the pulpit.

But Indianapolis wasn't big enough to contain Jones's voracious megalomania, and the ceaseless self-promotion wore thin within a few years. Rumors about the Temple's ceaseless fund-raising were spreading, and officials in city hall were beginning to look askance at those relentlessly advertised claims that Reverend Jones offered cures for cancer, arthritis, and heart disease.

Always alert to the first whiff of trouble, Jones suddenly had a religious epiphany. He announced to his startled congregation that God had visited him with a dire warning: nuclear holocaust was coming to destroy most of the world. Only two places would be safe havens for the righteous: Belo Horizonte, Brazil (which he visited on a "missionary" mission in 1962), and Ukiah, California, about a hundred miles north of San Francisco.

Ukiah being somewhat more convenient, Jones and a loyal crowd of followers—more than a hundred of them would make the journey—drove across country in 1965 in a caravan of cars and minibuses, with Jones's shiny black Cadillac at the front. It was the first proof that some people would follow him just about anywhere.

Jim Jones's ego was such that he acknowledged no role model save one: Father Divine, a fabulously wealthy inner-city black preacher, a Harlem-born charismatic who had amassed a huge following among poor blacks migrating into northern cities during the 1920s and '30s. Father Divine's "Kingdom of Heaven"—built around converted old downtown hotels where followers lived in communal ecstasy— was still thriving in the sixties when Jones started to build his own ministry. Jones correctly saw in Father Divine's Kingdom a brilliant amalgam of church, business, and political machine. To his followers, Father Divine was God. But to white urban power brokers, he was a black Caesar, a political genius who could swing an election in the Negro wards with a nod of his head.

In the late fifties Father Divine's wife, Sara, published a biography of her spouse, *Father Divine: Holy Husband*. In it she concluded that "if Father Divine were to die, mass suicide among the Negroes in his movement would almost certainly result . . . This would be the shame of America."

This sentiment thrilled Jones. In the early sixties, accompanied by his now-constant entourage, Jones had even traveled to Philadelphia for a personal meeting with Father Divine. He was bitterly disappointed when his hero was too decrepit to receive him.

Father Divine died in 1965, just as the People's Temple was relocating to find new opportunities in California. Jones waited impatiently for the mass suicide of stricken followers of Father Divine, but it did not occur. Worse, Father Divine's widow and some of his followers subsequently moved to the suburbs and lived a life of luxury. Father Divine himself was quickly forgotten except as a historical footnote.

Jones vowed that the same thing would never happen to him.

*   *   *

To Jones, the spotlight was not meant to be shared. Hardly missing a beat after the migration from Indiana to California, he quickly established a new Temple and made sure everybody knew who was its master. During angry sermons he would raise the Bible high above his head and dash it to the floor, screaming at his flock: "Too many people are looking at *this,* and not at *me!*"

No opportunity, no matter how melodramatic, was lost to dramatize "Father"—as he insisted on being called—as a great leader who was feared by unknown enemies of the Temple. Persecution was a constant undercurrent in his sermons. In 1968, when Rev. Martin Luther King, Jr. was assassinated, Jones horrified the congregation by staging a fake assassination attempt of himself, staggering onto the altar at Sunday service covered with chicken blood and claiming he had been shot. As the followers shrieked and gasped, Father convulsed, prayed—and sprang to his feet, miraculously recovered. The congregation roared in ecstasy.

Still, despite what God had told him about a haven from nuclear destruction, Jones again became restless in rugged Ukiah. Leaving behind a compound where selected followers were trained in survival skills, firearms, and self-defense, Jones once again moved the People's Temple, this time to San Francisco. There, he spent over a half-million dollars renovating a spacious old Masonic Temple on Geary Street in the heavily black Fillmore district, just up the block from the headquarters of the Black Panther Party. Hundreds of followers who had come with him moved into houses and apartments all around the new Temple and began pounding the pavements for new recruits.

It was in many ways a repeat of the experience in Indianapolis—but on a vastly larger scale and in the libertine environment of San Francisco in the seventies, where a large pool of young social idealists existed for recruiting.

The Temple soon became a major Fillmore attraction, with its foot-stomping, boisterous church services at which Jones preached damnation while curing the sick. Thousands of followers packed into the church on Sunday mornings. As never before, the Temple reached into the community with open arms, serving thousands of free meals a month, housing the poor in dormitories that provided pools of workers for Temple businesses. Jones set up a neighborhood health clinic that provided free screenings, VD treatment, tests for sickle-cell anemia. He also set up a drug-treatment clinic and instituted child-care services and senior citizens programs.

The indefatigable Jones joined community boards, networked with politicians and taught community organizing classes at night-school programs, recruiting idealistic new members all the while. As always, the neighborhood around the Temple blossomed with posters attesting to Father's powers. One described him as a "prophet, public school teacher, and governmental official" who "saves the lives of total strangers with his predictions" and "amazing healings" of diseases such as cancer. Flyers promised a "185-voice choir" and said at the bottom, "Free Banquet."

Financially, Jones was able to live high and travel in style, always surrounded by aides and bodyguards.

Politically, the payoff also was impressive. Word of the Temple's aggressive social programs and its exuberant brand of boisterous left-wing Christian activism spread among community leaders and in the local news media, whose glowing reports on the People's Temple brought in ever more followers and donations.

Jones consolidated his power like a ward boss lusting for the mayor's office. On issues of Jones's choosing, the Temple routinely generated massive letter-writing campaigns. Literally thousands of Temple protesters could be turned out on short notice for political demonstrations—or for a politician's rally. Candidates for state and city offices lined up for his support. During the 1976 presidential campaign he was visited by national political figures and had a private dinner with Rosalynn Carter, wife of the Democratic candidate. Closer to home, he managed to take over the local chapter of the NAACP by registering People's Temple membership en masse. He invited reporters to Temple services to experience the "joy," and he made large public contributions to First Amendment funds and other causes dear to journalists. He forged a valuable alliance with the city's leading black publisher, Carlton Goodlet, whose *Sun-Reporter* adopted Jim Jones as its favorite politician, white or black.

Jones's opinions on local issues were constantly publicized in the media. He was feted at testimonials and awards ceremonies for the Temple's social work. After a mass letter-writing campaign organized by the Temple, he was even named to the city Housing Authority Commission. In no time Jones dominated the powerful civic commission as Temple supporters packed the hearing room to lend their vocal support and shout down any murmur of dissent.

"This was a guy who could do no wrong," a local columnist said.

But spiritually, beneath the thunder of clapping hands and stomping feet and the blaze of spotlights and hype, there was something dreadfully wrong with the Jim Jones phenomenon. Amazingly, the horror stories stayed hidden until it was too late.

There had always been talk of Jones's prodigious sexual appetite, which he did little to conceal. Bisexual by inclination, he boasted to associates that he could have several sexual partners and still find the urge to masturbate as much as a dozen times a day. Less publicly, he stalked the streets of the Haight-Ashbury and downtown San Francisco at night looking for male "recruits" among the new hordes of disaffiliated youths who had come to the city. One minute he could be snorting cocaine and connecting with a male prostitute in an adult movie theater—he was in fact arrested for this in 1973, but charges were quietly dropped—and the next he could be seen railing from the Temple's pulpit against the horrors of sexual license.

Demanding sexual abstinence among his followers even while he maintained what some whispered was a "harem" of young women from their ranks—all of them, it was noted, were white—Jones worked to weaken marriages within the congregation. When sex was allowed, Jones had to approve it. Children were kept from parents' company as much as possible. As family structures weakened, personal property became easier to part with. Entire households turned over everything to the Temple.

Nevertheless, like all leaders of cults, he was especially adept at appealing to confused and idealistic young people with college educations and a pipeline into family finances. New believers flocked in. As they did, they were folded into an organization in which nothing was left to chance, where all impulses led to control over people's words, movements, and ideas.

Church services took on a lurid theatricality, part tent revival, part New Left political rally, performed in bright lights on an altar that resembled a trade-show stage. His face puffy from drugs and booze, his cheeks and forehead perpetually wet with sweat, his eyes concealed behind dark aviator sunglasses, his hair dyed jet-black and plastered over his forehead, his limbs akimbo in a flowing red robe, a microphone grasped in one hand and a Bible in the other, Jones had become almost a caricature of a Bible-thumping shyster. But his congregation thought he was God.

He employed a theatrical makeup expert who powdered his face and rouged his cheeks, and even used eyebrow pencil to fill out his sideburns to resemble Elvis Presley's. Impostors were hired to fake being cured, even putting on ghoul faces to stage demonic-possession seizures to allow Jones to exorcize the beast.

Jones's spy network, already adept at gathering confidential information that Jones could use from the pulpit, intensified its intelligence gathering to maintain dossiers on the habits, quirks, and personal finances of hundreds of followers, at times riffling their trash or burglarizing apartments.

From the beginning of his ministry Jones understood the power of group fear. He established "interrogation committees" within the congregation, supposedly to listen to complaints, but staffed with spies who promptly prepared reports on dissenters. At the weekly—and mandatory—catharsis sessions, which went on until people were bleary-eyed and exhausted in the early morning hours, "troublemakers" were paddled with wooden boards and sometimes severely beaten by Jones's surly aides. Chastened miscreants were required to shout, "Thank you, Father!"

As time went on, the talk of persecution and martyrdom intensified. Always making up his theology as he went along, Jones expounded on a new theory that he called "Translation," in which the entire congregation would ultimately die together, and afterward be transported as a group to another planet to spend eternity in bliss with their leader. Jones, who had to be called "Father" or "Dad" in every sentence addressed to him, began compiling a list of those suspected of lacking sufficient enthusiasm about dying. From the pulpit he would identify culprits, screaming: "The names I have just read are people who can't be trusted yet!" These were people, he said, not yet "fully ready" to die for "the cause."

In her book *Six Years With God,* a woman named Jeannie Mills, who finally defected from Jones's flock, described how Father instilled in his flock the acceptance of group death. "I want to take a vote today to find out how dedicated you all are." Jones would intone from the altar that life was a "bore." How many people, he would ask, "would be willing to take your own lives now to keep the church from being discredited?"

Betrayal lurked everywhere, he declared. The People's Temple, he stressed, was a family. When tyranny came, only Father could provide protection. There was renewed talk of finding a new place to escape persecution. In the mid-seventies Jones intensified work on a major fund-raising drive to help the Temple establish itself in a safe haven, in a socialist utopia free from betrayal and the threat of nuclear holocaust.

With so much coming at them all the time, Jones's followers adopted a standard refrain to explain the bewildering mess they had gotten themselves so joyfully into:

"Dad knows best," they told each other.

By 1977, with local news accounts unquestioningly accepting Jones's claim that the People's Temple had 20,000 members—actually, the number was less than 3,000—"Dad" was having some problems. For the first time, a number of followers—disgusted by the beatings, the depravity, and the worsening messianic delusions of Jones himself—began quietly leaving the church. At first they felt alone, often ashamed of the gullibility that had led them to give all to the cult. But in time the defectors began to seek each other out and compare notes. They decided the time had come to go public with allegations that Jones's hold over many of his followers was based on fear, fraud, and chicanery.

Among the defectors were a white couple named

Elmer and Deanna Myrtle, who with their five children had been members of the Temple from 1969 until 1975. Deanna Myrtle was a former Seventh Day Adventist; her husband was a civil rights activist who had marched with Dr. King at Selma. They joined the Temple because of a mutual belief in what they called "apostolic socialism," signed over to Jones their life savings and $50,000 worth of real estate and, like other followers, complied with Jones's bizarre demands that they sign false "confession" forms. They fled when they realized that Jones was serious about mass suicide. The Myrtles so completely repudiated their past that they even changed their names, to Al and Jeannie Mills.

In an affidavit, the Millses said Jim Jones had a "strange power" over his flock, which they attributed partly to "fear, guilt, and extreme fatigue" instilled at all-night services and catharsis sessions. "We rationalized the punishments and disciplines because we believed that [Jones] was God and could do no wrong," Jeannie Mills later wrote. "We sincerely believed that he would always take care of us."

After leaving the Temple, people like the Millses all reported receiving anonymous threats and frequent unwanted at-home visits from church "counselors" demanding their return. Some reported beatings and said their houses were burglarized.

But Jones was the one with the public relations steamroller. Now organized into a group called Concerned Relatives, the defectors—along with relatives of followers who claimed Jones was holding people hostage in a messianic cult—had no luck getting a hearing from news organizations like the San Francisco *Chronicle,* which had invested years of positive coverage in Jim Jones as a dedicated community leader and social activist and had no inclination to see its accolades exposed as hype.

However, they did get the attention of a reporter named Marshall Kildruff, preparing an article on the People's Temple for *New West* magazine. Kildruff stubbornly began peeling away the public relations facade that Jones had built and uncovering the layers of fraud, terror, and intimidation that lay at the center of Jones's hold over his flock.

Jones reacted predictably when his spies told him what the reporter was up to. Temple members churned out hundreds of letters to the magazine's advertisers; *New West*'s editorial offices were burglarized; a rough draft of the Kildruff article was stolen.

Nevertheless, the *New West* exposé ran in August 1977, and detailed allegations that Jones routinely committed fraud, child abuse, assault, and criminal extortion in the operations of the People's Temple. The article created a public furor. Two weeks later, alarmed city officials were relieved to receive a letter from Jim Jones in which he resigned his post on the Housing Authority. The letter was postmarked "Cooperative Republic of Guyana."

As always, Jones got out of town one step ahead of the sheriff. The fund-raising campaign to establish a socialist commune away from prying eyes, in a place where his control could be absolute, had been spectacularly successful. Jones had over a million dollars to build his new world.

After investigating and ruling out locations in Kenya and Cuba, he had settled on a site in a country few people could even locate on a map—Guyana, a former British colony wedged on the Atlantic Coast of South America between Venezuela and Brazil. Guyana's black-majority Marxist government was receptive to the propaganda value posed by the defection of a group of Americans, most of them blacks fleeing U.S. imperialist tyranny. It also helped that their leader, Jones, had lots of money to spread around.

"The People's Temple in Guyana intends to be an agricultural mission," Jones had said when plans were first announced a few years before the publicity turned sour. Its purpose was to produce food to feed the hungry.

The colony was set up under the supervision of Jim and Marceline's natural son Stephan, now seventeen years old. In 1977, Stephan had led the initial contingent of about fifty People's Temple settlers to their new socialist utopia on 3,800 desolate acres in the thick jungle near the Venezuela border, deep within the vast rain forest covering the northwest part of the country, 150 miles from the nearest significant settlement, the capital, Georgetown. For many months they toiled from dawn to midnight hacking away brush and felling hardwood trees to clear the ground, plow the fields, and begin raising the tin-roofed structures that would house the dormitories, bunkhouses, sheds, and recreational halls of a primitive settlement, first called the Jonestown Agricultural and Medical Mission and then, simply, Jonestown.

In ensuing months the settlers were joined by others—including a number of "troublemakers" whom Jones thought needed more intensive indoctrination.

Hundreds of elderly followers were among the first new arrivals.

During the latter part of 1977—often before their friends and relatives realized what was happening—most of the Temple residents in San Francisco were making plans to join their colleagues in Jonestown. By the end of the year, as press accounts back home followed up on the *New West* exposé and documented even more abuses at the Temple, the congregation had effectively left San Francisco, resettling en masse to a remote, forlorn work camp in Guyana. By early 1978 even the once-enthralled San Francisco *Chronicle* had seen the light, harshly describing Jonestown as a "jungle outpost" where "the Rev. Jim Jones orders public beatings, maintains a squad of fifty armed guards, and has involved his 1,100 followers in a threat of mass suicide."

Now squarely on the defensive, even from thousands of miles away, the People's Temple publicity apparatus fired back from the jungle. In May 1978 the Temple flooded U.S. news outlets with press releases ridiculing Jones's critics as a "sordid crew" of malcontents, perverts, embezzlers, and child abusers who had been expelled from the church and were now seeking revenge. Included with the statement were confession forms.

In the summer, as the Concerned Relatives stepped up pressure to do something about the suicide threats they claimed to be hearing from Jonestown, another press release denounced a "politically motivated conspiracy" to destroy the church. The statement added, "We will resist actively, putting our lives on the line" to defend the Jonestown settlement. "This has been the unanimous vote of the collective community."

Jones had hired as an attorney the Kennedy assassination conspiracy theorist Mark Lane. In September, Lane held a press conference to denounce what he called "a conspiracy to destroy the People's Temple, Jonestown, and Jim Jones."

Other than such publicity salvos, there was little information at all from Jonestown, where the only regular communications links were mail and short-wave radio. All mail and shortwave transmissions to and from the jungle outpost were carefully monitored by Jones's ever-vigilant staff.

Jonestown was in fact a plantation ruled by Jones and his white aides, with the black majority in the fields all day under tropical heat, carefully supervised by guards who took notes of attitudes and comments. The workday began at seven A.M. and lasted till sunset, followed by mandatory meetings in the open-air pavilion that went on beyond the point of exhaustion till two or three A.M. Thanks to its isolation and the terms of its friendly lease with Guyanese authorities, Jonestown was essentially an autonomous dictatorship that maintained its own police force, judicial system, jail, schools, health care, and defense. There was no appeal of Jones's dictates.

Promotional brochures sent to members lingering in California had depicted a tropical paradise with palm trees and happy faces. They did not show the security force—deceptively named the Learning Crew—whose hundred thuglike members wielded power like a banana-republic goon squad and carried semiautomatic rifles, shotguns and deadly spring-loaded crossbows. Like Jones, the Learning Crew also had access to liquor, quality imported food, and their choice of sexual partners, male or female, willing or not.

Having no need now to impress outside observers, Jones consolidated control over this primitive police state where people were fed food that sometimes crawled with maggots, and toiled relentlessly under appalling sanitary conditions. Children developed ringworm, lice, and infections.

Social conditions were no better. With his authority absolute, Jones destroyed what little was left of family cohesion, segregating men and women in separate dorms, with children housed away from parents.

For any violation of these and myriad other rules, punishment was more swift and severe than ever. Beatings with fists and straps were routinely administered. Another form of punishment was a "stretching," in which four camp guards would grab a miscreant by each leg and arm and pull until unconsciousness arrived. Female offenders were beaten and then forced to strip and stand naked in public, or engage in oral sex in front of the congregation. If a married couple was discovered in private conversation, the woman—or the couple's teenage daughter, if they had one—could be forced to masturbate in front of the group.

Though punishments now occurred all day long, the most serious offenses were dealt with at nightly camp meetings, where Jones supervised from a wooden "throne" on an altarlike platform at the center of the open-sided camp pavilion where meals were served. Sometimes, offenders were dragged in unconscious—after being beaten or sometimes drugged—and then "resurrected" by Jones. For offenses as trivial as forgetting to call Jones "Father," children could be locked into wooden boxes for weeks on end, or forced to eat hot peppers, vomit, and eat that. When the children were beaten, Jones himself usually joined in with a few well-aimed kicks and slaps, and held the microphone to broadcast their screams on loudspeakers installed all over the compound: "I'm sorry Father! I'm sorry, Father!" Beaten, held underwater, terrified with live snakes at their faces, children were required to say, "Thank you, Father."

During the nightly meetings, while he harangued the congregation for hours, Jones also read "news reports" from home that painted a bleak picture of deteriorating life in the U.S., including word that Los Angeles was being evacuated in anticipation of racial warfare.

All the while, Father's grasp of reality was worsening on a steady diet of amphetamines and quaaludes. At the same time, psychoactive drugs commonly used in mental hospitals to calm severely ill patients were routinely administered to Jonestown "troublemakers," including children, who were confined to a shacklike psycho ward called the ECU—extended care unit.

Yet escape was not a viable option. Day and night, armed guards patrolled the perimeters to discourage anyone foolhardy enough to try to flee into the dense jungle. Three times a day the entire camp population was required to assemble for roll calls.

Nor was there any sign of rescue. Outside visitors were discouraged, but the few who did obtain permission to visit the jungle outpost saw only happy faces in the fields and at the playground, sawmill, and basketball court. Before they were escorted out, visitors enjoyed a special dinner, always with entertainment by the camp choir, band, and children's chorus.

Given the protection Jonestown received from the Guyanese government, the U.S. Embassy in the capital of Georgetown was not inclined to aggressively investigate complaints coming from California. An embassy cable noted the "serious allegations" about conditions at Jonestown, but warned that unannounced surprise visits were impossible since "a minimum of two to three days" was needed to get access to the camp.

Another diplomat later said there was no clear understanding of what Jonestown was. "We thought they were something like Quakers," he said.

Hopelessly isolated, manipulated into a state of irrationality by Jones's unbending barrages of fear and paranoia, the Jonestown community was ready to die.

Macabre "White Night" drills—preparations for mass suicide—became a routine part of life. Without warning, usually in the hours just before dawn, camp sirens would scream as loudspeakers bellowed, "Alert! Alert!" Silently, the men, women, and children of Jonestown would awake, dress, and fall out to assemble at the pavilion, where a wild-eyed Jones would be ranting from his throne, bathed in white light. "There are CIA mercenaries out there waiting to destroy us," he would shriek, waving his arm at the dark jungle all around them.

Dutifully at White Nights, everybody drank cups of a fruit-flavored beverage that Jones said was poison. There were forty-three White Nights during the last year in the jungle. On every occasion but the last, the residents of Jonestown drank the liquid and were told to go back to bed, that it was "just a drill."

Alarmed by reports from the Concerned Relatives and others, a crusading Democratic congressman from San Mateo County, Leo Ryan, decided to get some answers late in 1978.

Lauded by supporters as a liberal reformer with a social conscience, but derided by critics as a fuzzy-minded publicity seeker, the fifty-three-year-old Ryan used his membership on the House Foreign Affairs Committee to arrange a fact-finding trip to Guyana to look into what he called the potential "hijacking of a thousand people." If reports were true that people were being held there against their will, Ryan said, he would escort them home.

The trip was set for November. Ryan would not come back alive.

Ryan tried to enlist national news organizations to accompany him on his fact-finding trip to the jungle colony. In all, eight journalists signed on, among them reporters for the *Washington Post,* NBC News, and the San Francisco *Chronicle.* The core of the delegation consisted of Ryan, his assistant Jacqueline Speier, and a House aide named James Schollaert. They would also be accompanied by thirteen representatives of the Concerned Relatives.

From its first days, the Jonestown settlement's medical officer was Dr. Larry Schacht, a physician whose professional education had been financed by People's Temple. As the Ryan delegation was in the air en route to Guyana, Dr. Schacht was busy in the camp pharmacy, unpacking a newly arrived shipment of a chemical that Jones had ordered. It was liquid cyanide.

The visiting Americans arrived at the airport near Georgetown on November 15, 1978. But they had to cool their heels in the capital for a few days until permission came from Guyanese authorities to make the trip north to Jonestown. While they waited, there was an unmistakable signal that their presence was not welcomed, when an aide to Jones arrived at the Georgetown hotel where the Americans were staying to hand Ryan a petition signed by six hundred Jonestown residents demanding that the intruders go home and leave them alone.

Accompanied by *Washington Post* reporter Charles Krause, Ryan stalked over to the office the People's Temple maintained in Georgetown at 41 Lamaha Gardens. "I'm Leo Ryan, the bad guy," he announced. "Does anybody want to talk?"

No one did. He was told that Jones was not available for interviews either. Back at his hotel, Ryan told reporters that he was going up to Jonestown whether he was welcome or not. On Friday morning, when governmental permission was finally granted for the trip, lawyers Mark Lane and Charles Garry, representing People's Temple in Georgetown, phoned Jones at the compound to urge him to receive the visitors. Garry told Jones, "You can tell the Congress of the United States, the press, and the relatives to fuck themselves. If you do that, it's the end of the ball game. The other alternative is to let them in and prove to the world that these people criticizing you are crazy."

Jones finally agreed to receive the delegation, but he wasn't happy about it.

With visitors coming, word was passed within the Jonestown commune that everyone was to be on their best behavior. The loudspeakers broadcast a warning: "If you mess up, you will get the severest punishment."

The Ryan delegation left that afternoon in a chartered twin-engine plane that had room for only nineteen passengers. On board with the congressman were his two aides, nine journalists, a U.S. Embassy officer, Richard Dwyer, a representative from the Guyanese government, and four of the Concerned Relatives. The trip to Jonestown was an hour-long flight over an impenetrable canopy of jungle.

Around four o'clock the plane bumped down on the airstrip, which was little more than a wide gravel path and a tin shed. Beside it was a sleepy village called Port Kaituma, on the edge of the jungle, six miles down a dirt road from Jonestown. The plane was met by a yellow truck containing six Temple members.

When they arrived at the compound, Krause was taken with the primitive scene that unfolded before them. He thought it looked like something out of *Gone With the Wind:* "Old black women were baking bread in the bakery, people were washing clothes in the laundry, black and white children were chasing each other in the little park, and long lines of people, mostly black, were waiting for their suppers." Initially, he thought the camp seemed both "peaceful" and "bucolic."

Marceline Jones received the delegation graciously, ushering them to a long wooden dining table at the head of the pavilion. There they were introduced to a smiling Jim Jones, clad in neat khaki pants and a sport shirt, wearing his trademark dark sunglasses.

While the NBC crew set up for an interview with Jones, Ryan wandered off to speak casually with some of the residents. Dinner was both ample and delicious, the visitors discovered to their surprise: hot pork sandwiches, collard greens, and potato salad, served on plastic trays.

After the meal, the lights dimmed. The Jonestown band struck up the Guyanese national anthem, followed by "America the Beautiful." Then the visitors sat back for two hours of entertainment that included the huge People's Temple choir, as well as dancing by groups of children.

Taking it in, Ryan began to wonder if the dire reports about conditions he had been hearing from the Concerned Relatives had been gross exaggerations. When asked to rise and say a few words after the show, the congressman seemed favorably impressed.

"Despite the charges I've heard about Jonestown, I am sure that there are people here this evening who believe that this is the best thing that ever happened to them in their whole lives," he said. When he was finished speaking, the seven hundred Jonestown residents crowded into the pavilion rose to give him a rousing ovation.

But Ryan wasn't finished. "I want to pull no punches. This is a congressional inquiry."

Jones, fortified by a heavy dose of amphetamines, couldn't leave well enough alone. Speaking with reporters after dinner, his eyes hidden behind the sun-glasses despite the darkness that had fallen, he became defensive and combative. "They say I want power," he said bitterly, waving a ring-studded hand at the multitudes of smiling followers. "What kind of power do I have, walking down the path to my little old seniors? I hate power. I hate money. All I want is peace. I'm not worried about my image." But the outside criticisms of Jonestown must stop, he warned abruptly. "If we could just stop it! But if we don't, I don't know what's going to happen to twelve hundred lives here."

The visitors were suddenly asked to leave and re-turn for breakfast the next day, Saturday. They were driven back to the airstrip, where they spent the night in sleeping bags.

Returning the next morning, they noticed a palpa-ble difference in the atmosphere at the camp, as if they had already overstayed their tentative welcome. After breakfast, reporters wandering around found that despite the jungle heat, some of the barracks were locked tight, the shades tightly drawn over their windows. Guards curtly informed them that the peo-ple inside were afraid of harm from the visitors.

But the reporters managed to gain access to one of the barracks buildings. Inside they discovered more than a hundred bunk beds, stacked two and three high, occupied by old black people. One of the el-derly residents, Edith Parks, a nurse, anxiously whis-pered to a reporter that she would like to leave with him. Her son, daughter-in-law, and three grandchil-dren were also in the compound, she confided.

The reporters sought out Jones, whose attempts to put the best face on things were unraveling even as the NBC camera rolled. Jones was red-eyed, haggard, and extremely agitated. NBC correspondent Don Harris asked him about rumors—which could now be clearly verified by the visitors—that the compound was patrolled by heavily armed guards to prevent people from leaving.

"A bold-faced lie!" Jones shouted, rapidly losing control. "It seems like we are defeated by lies! I'm defeated! I might as well die." As the television camera zoomed in on his face, he railed about conspiracies and threats. "I wish somebody had shot me dead," he cried. "Now we've substituted the media smear for assassination!"

Harris was astonished. The man seemed to be coming apart in front of him, on camera. Pressing the advantage, he handed Jones a handwritten note that had been given him by one of the residents, asking to be rescued.

"People play games, friend," Jones retorted, crumbling the note in disgust. "They lie. What can I do with liars?" Eyes darting, panic flushing his face, he looked like a trapped animal. "Are you people going to leave us? I just beg you, please leave us! Anybody that wants to go can get out of here. They come and go all the time. The more that leave, the less responsibility we have. Who in hell wants people?"

Clouds were piling up ominously above the trees. The wind picked up. A slight drizzle was falling as Ryan stepped up to Jones. With the congressman was a nervous resident who said he wanted to get out with his children. "There's a family of six that wants to leave," Ryan told Jones. In fact, fifteen people in all had asked Ryan's delegation to take them from Jonestown. Ryan was concerned now, worried that the nineteen-passenger plane sitting back at the airstrip would be inadequate.

Jones exploded. "I feel betrayed! It never stops!" But he offered to provide money to transport out anyone who wanted to leave. "American dollars!" he was screaming, but guards had already moved to herd the delegation toward the truck that would take them to the airstrip.

Jones accosted Mrs. Parks, who had been with him since Indianapolis and who looked at her leader with great sadness in her eyes. "You're not the man I knew," she said with pity.

"Don't do this to me, Edie," Jones pleaded. "Wait until the congressman goes and then I'll give you the money and your passports."

"No," the old woman said, summoning her courage. "This is our chance. We're going."

There was a commotion as her son tried to find a child who had wandered off. The rain was falling heavily now, pounding on the leaves. Suddenly, a burly guard grabbed Ryan from behind and held a long knife to his throat.

"Congressman Ryan, you are a motherfucker," said the assailant as some of the terrified residents standing by cheered nervously.

Aghast, the two lawyers, Lane and Garry, struggled with the guard, forcing him to release the startled Ryan. In the scuffle, the guard's hand was slashed. Blood splattered on Ryan's white shirt.

A tense truce was worked out. The fifteen who had approached the delegation would be allowed to leave. After three P.M. a dump truck was provided to carry the Ryan party and the fifteen defectors back to the airstrip, where they would be ferried by plane to Georgetown.

But as the truck started out of the camp, one of Jones's top aides, Larry Layton, jumped on board. His presence frightened the defectors crowded into the well of the truck. "He'll kill us!" one cried. Worried about nightfall coming before the plane could get everyone back to the capital, Ryan tried to calm the group as the truck lumbered down the rutted jungle road in low gear, its wheels churning through mud from the torrential downpour.

The truck reached the airstrip around 4:30 P.M. The plane was not there.

Hoping to film another interview with Ryan at the airstrip while they waited for the plane, NBC's Don Harris helped his crew to set up as the group, still rattled by the attack on Ryan, milled around watching the gray sky drain of light. A photographer from the San Francisco *Examiner* unpacked his camera and began snapping more pictures.

With great relief, the group saw the nineteen-seat twin-engine Otter appear over the treetops. Behind it was another aircraft, a six-seat Cessna. One after the other the rescue planes landed and bounced up to the tarmac in front of the shack.

With clipboards in hand, Ryan and his aide Jackie Speier went about organizing the loading of passengers, assigning seats and designating those who would have to wait for the next trip.

The Cessna was loaded first. Ryan was standing back by the Otter, helping others to board.

Layton insisted that Ryan get on board the first plane. There was a shout from the group. A tractor pulling a flatbed trailer drove up and parked between the two planes. Three of Jones's guards hopped off the trailer and raised automatic weapons.

Without a word of warning, they began firing.

In a panic, the bystanders ran or hit the ground. Dwyer, the Guyanese representative, was shot. Edith Parks's daughter Patricia slumped beside the door of the Otter, her head blown apart by bullets. The gunmen fired point-blank at *Chronicle* photographer Greg Robinson, who was still snapping pictures when he fell dead.

Chronicle reporter Ron Javers took a bullet in the shoulder and also went down. *Washington Post* reporter Charles Krause was shot in the hip.

Methodically, the gunmen moved around the plane, where the NBC cameraman, Rob Brown, had found a place to keep filming. He was hit in the leg and crumpled beside his camera. One of Jones's guards strode up to him, calmly pressed the barrel of his rifle at his temple and fired.

Futilely seeking refuge behind the fat tires of one of the planes, Ryan and Harris were riddled with bullets. Finishing them off, a gunmen stepped up to the two men and blasted them both in the face. For good measure, they did the same to Robinson, already dead. Then the gunmen got back on the trailer and drove off.

The Cessna with survivors on board managed to take off. The Otter was disabled by gunfire. All around it lay the dead—Ryan, Harris, Brown, Robinson, and a Jonestown defector—and the eleven others who had been wounded. Shivering, crying in pain, they would spend the night on the ground before a plane arrived to take them to Georgetown at daylight.

* * *

As the carnage was raging at the airstrip six miles away, Jones furiously ordered a night of unspeakable horror to begin. The two outside lawyers on the scene with Jones—the fifty-one-year-old Lane and his seventy-two-year-old colleague Garry—had no idea of what had occurred at the airstrip. Shaken by the attack on Ryan before he had left, they were anxiously planning to depart Jonestown the next morning.

An aide to Jones approached them. "Father wants to see you."

They were taken to a clearing where they found Jones, disheveled and frantic, crying on a bench.

"This is terrible, terrible," he said. He tried to explain that three gunmen from Jonestown had gone off in pursuit of the Ryan delegation and he didn't know what they might do. "They love me and they may do something that will reflect badly on me," he sobbed. "They're going to shoot at the people and their planes. They want to kill somebody . . . they've taken every gun in the place!"

Jones was lying. He had ordered the assault. He also had ordered the final White Night. Just then the compound's dreaded loudspeakers boomed to life. "Alert! Alert! Alert!"

This time it was not a drill. Instructions were passed for everyone to wear their best clothes.

Ignoring the commotion, Jones stared morosely at the two worried lawyers. "Feeling is running very high against you," he said, getting up and walking toward the pavilion. "I can't say what might happen at the meeting." He ordered the lawyers to go to a guest cottage and stay there until further notice. As they passed a porch of a bungalow, they encountered a guard who told them simply, "We are going to die."

Out of the fetid dorms to where they had been confined, dutifully filed the followers of Jim Jones. As they had done so many times before, they silently filed into the pavilion area as the loudspeakers screeched.

In the kitchen, Stanley Clayton, a cook, had been preparing dinner when the loudspeakers boomed the alert. By now, White Nights were routine occurrences. He was stirring a vat of black-eyed peas when armed guards barged in and ordered him to go to the pavilion with the others. At once, he knew that this was no drill.

Jones had taken his place on his throne, which sat in the center of the open-sided pavilion on a wooden platform that he called the "high altar." As usual, he held a microphone to address his flock. On a table beside him was a tape recorder that he would use to save his final sermon for posterity.

At first there was a little commotion around Jones as top aides ascertained his intentions. At various escape points on walkways leading to the pavilion, armed guards silently took position. The two lawyers watched the activity with a growing sense of peril.

Lane managed to stop a guard, who told him that Jones had ordered a mass suicide to protest "racism" and "fascism." This would not be a drill, he said.

"Then Charles and I will write about what you do, the history of what you believed in," Lane replied.

"Fine," said the guard.

Assessing the situation, the lawyers dashed out of

the cottage and hid in the jungle. Both would escape with their lives.

From the high altar, his speech starting to slur as the community filed into the staging area, Jones announced that the end of the journey had come.

"I want my babies first," he said. "Take my babies and children first."

Nearby on a long dining table nurses filled syringes with cyanide, to squirt the poison into the mouths of small children. Guards now ringed Jones's place on the high altar. Some raised crossbows, cocked taut and ready.

As the congregation filled in the spaces around the stage, more than a thousand people in all, a senior aide's orders to the guards resonated on the loudspeakers: "If you see anyone doing a suspicious or treacherous act, if you see anyone trying to leave, I want them shot."

Jones's voice then was heard. "Let's don't fight one another. Let's do it right." He kept a finger on his tape recorder, switching it on and off, editing himself as he rambled.

"In spite of all I've tried, a handful of people with their lies have made our lives impossible," he said, decrying them for "the betrayal of the century."

The old magic was working. Some of the congregation screamed in religious ecstasy. Others danced feverishly in the aisles. Many sang.

"What's going to happen in a matter of a few minutes is that one of those people on the plane is going to shoot the pilot," he said, adding that he hadn't planned it that way. There would be retaliation, he warned. "They'll parachute in here on us."

He spoke of "so many, many pressures on my brain," because of the "treasonous" behavior. Then he told them to drink the poison: "Take the potion like they used to take in ancient Greece, and step over quietly," he said, calling it a "revolutionary" act. "They're now going back to tell more lies, which means more congressmen," he warned. Again he prodded them to die. "Take my babies and children first."

Jones spiraled inexorably into the mad helix. The event, so well-rehearsed, had assumed a momentum of its own. In the medical tent near the pavilion, Dr. Schacht supervised the preparation of a big washtub of red-colored Fla-Vor-Aid. He poured in cyanide from big pharmacy bottles.

Jones railed on, "Anybody that has any dissenting opinion, please speak."

Surprisingly, someone did, asking why the children had to die first.

"If the children are left, we're going to have them butchered," Jones responded.

Someone else asked, Couldn't they leave the jungle and find a new home farther away?

Jones said the die was cast. "It's too late. They've gone with the guns." Ryan and others were dead! Enemies were moving through the jungle, coming by air to take Jonestown and avenge the deaths.

A young mother strode up to the edge of the altar and said, "I look at all the babies, and I think they deserve to live."

Jones snapped off the tape recorder and fixed her with a cold stare. "I'm going to see that you die," he said.

Then Dr. Schacht and a nurse moved into view in

the pavilion as the battered washtub was carried in and placed on a table. Beside the tub were arranged the syringes and paper cups. Security guards shouted orders. Compliantly, as always, the congregation silently formed a line.

"Please get us some medication," Jones exhorted them. "It's simple. There's no convulsions with it."

Jones handed the microphone to an excited man who had pushed his way through the crowd to the high altar. "I'm ready to go," he screamed in eerie joy. "If you tell us we have to give our lives now, we're ready. All the rest of the sisters and brothers are with us!"

This was not exactly the case. There was in fact some grumbling from the crowd. But as usual, troublemakers were quickly identified by guards and isolated. Some were taken aside, beaten in the shadows of the jungle, and then roughly pushed back into place in line. The lightning suppression strategy worked well. Murmurs of protest died on the wind.

"Hurry!" Jones shrieked madly on the loudspeakers. "Hurry, my children! It's just something to put you to rest . . . Children, it will not hurt!"

As the men, women, and children who had followed him to the jungle shuffled forward for their lethal communion, Jones stood red-faced and wild-eyed, bathed in harsh bright light before his throne. "I tried to keep this from happening!" he moaned. "Now I don't think we should sit here and take any more time for our children to be endangered."

The first to drink the poison was a young mother with a little girl in her arms. She held the cup filled with the sugar-flavored poison to her child's lips and the child daintily sipped a little. Then the mother drank the rest. They wandered off into a cleared area, beyond the glaring penumbra of the floodlights, and sat quietly on the ground. In a few minutes their bodies shook with convulsions; a bloody foam formed on their mouths. The woman screamed and jerked violently, and then she was still. The child burrowed close to her mother, whimpered a little, and died.

Listlessly, the queue of the doomed filed along the table, hands mechanically dipping cups into vats of death. From the gathering darkness hellish screams rose in crescendo.

Darkness brought salvation to a few Jonestown residents who fled into the jungle and watched the grotesque tableau from hiding places. But they were only a handful. Most went blindly to their deaths, some of them shouting praise to their leader as they died, some hugging each other and saying calm good-byes before they drank. A few had to be prodded to drink. Sometimes a gun had to be used as persuasion. The nurses used the syringes to force the poison into the throats of crying babies.

As they drank, the doomed filed silently out of the pavilion and found space in clearings, where they were directed to lie facedown in long rows. One after the other the bodies convulsed and then were still. Using the toes of their boots, guards worked to keep the rows of the dead lined up neatly.

His voice hoarse, his mouth dry, his clothing soaked and stinking with amphetamine sweat, Jones raved in the spotlight as the hollow faces of the dying faded from the light. "I don't know what else to say to these people," he croaked, as if addressing himself. "To me, death is not a fearful thing."

The wails of the dying annoyed him, especially the crying of children. "Let's get it done! Let's get done!" he cried impatiently. "We tried to find a new beginning, but it's too late."

"Are we black, proud, and socialist?" the white preacher demanded, his eyes blazing. "Or what are we?"

The long night crept quietly over the death camp. As dawn finally streaked the sky, the only sounds were the shrieks of birds and the chatter of wild monkeys in the trees. Jonestown had died.

With daylight, Guyanese troops could be seen in the thick camouflage of foliage at the perimeter of Jonestown. Rifles ready, expecting armed resistance from the settlers, they moved cautiously into the camp. But there was no resistance from the corpses, stacked like firewood, already bloated and putrefying in the fierce morning heat. In all, there were 914 bodies on the ground, 276 of them children.

Only a few had been spared the indignities of a wretched death by poison, Jim Jones and his wife prominent among them. They had been shot. The soldiers found Jones, faceup, his eyes open, on the altar where he had killed himself with a single bullet to the right temple.

In time the shocked headlines faded. The jungle reclaimed Jonestown as its own. But somewhere still in there is a wooden sign that Jones himself had nailed on a beam above the altar, which displayed the words of the philosopher George Santayana: "Those who cannot remember the past are condemned to repeat it."

CHAPTER THREE

Gordon Kahl

Nearing his mid-fifties, Gordon Weldell Kahl was hardly an impressive figure—about five feet seven inches, running to fat on his stocky build, balding, with a fringe of closely trimmed gray hair. At first glance he might resemble a friendly grocer—but more careful study would show a hardness of the eyes, the tiny omnipresent sneer, the detached glare not of a grocer but of perhaps a retired Nazi death-camp guard.

Still, Gordon wasn't the sort of man you'd expect to find commemorated on T-shirts and bumper stickers. It was a bit disconcerting to connect that stolid round face with the baseball caps proclaiming "Go, Gordie, Go!" that sprouted all over the heartland of midwestern America after Gordon Kahl, professional patriot, killed those cops and ran for it.

"At last! We Have a Hero! Gordon Kahl, the First American Hero of the Second American Revolution," right-wing militant propaganda crowed in the aftermath of Gordon's spectacular 1983 standoff with the authorities.

An "Ode to Gordon Kahl" was published in dozens of neo-Nazi and other far-right newspapers, and called his death a heroic struggle, comparing him to Davy Crockett. "A soldier of our race has died," the song said.

There was even a ballad recorded and distributed to radio stations throughout the Farm Belt. It warns the federal government "just what happens when you mess with Freedom Fighter Gordon Kahl."

Gordon Kahl lived modestly and died spectacularly. To members of the small racist underground group he helped to lead to prominence, he was nothing less than the herald of Armageddon.

For years, Kahl preached his message of hate and revenge to people gripped in an intellectual isolation that belied the physical boundlessness of open prairie and wheat fields on which they lived. Jewish conspiracies to control the world through Moscow; prison camps being built by the U.S. government to confine millions of American patriots on the Arizona desert; Russian troops massed below the Rio Grande; MIG fighters training over Mexico; Vietcong guerrillas creeping through Texas—all were grist for the mill. Belief in one outlandish plot easily led to belief in them all. What was left was pure-grain paranoia.

Far-right populist agitators like Kahl had a standard and exhausting genealogy of villainy in America's farmland. The nearest line went through the regional bankers, the after-shave-lotion-scented swindlers at the savings and loan on Main Street who held the farmer's burgeoning debts and orchestrated the waves of foreclosures sweeping the Farm Belt during the 1980s. It then ran to their perfidious masters on Wall Street, laced up through the Federal Reserve Board to the dupes in the White House and Capitol Hill, lopped into the international Communist conspiracy, and tied the knot at the perpetrators of the diabolical master plot to wreck the American way of life. These masterminds were, of course, the Jews.

Since the late nineteenth century, similar conspiracy sentiments have sometimes found fertile ground in the aggrieved American Farm Belt, but the farm crisis of the 1980s—when an economic way of life was endangered by soaring debt and unrealized expectations—was a particularly propitious time for such sentiments. And Gordon Kahl was a master at exploiting the dark side of nativist American populism, even in death.

Despite the hate and contempt for outsiders constantly simmering just beneath his placid surface, Gordon Kahl usually managed to exhibit a natural midwestern gregariousness. He was a good talker, but more importantly, an attentive listener—an amiable fellow who could alight from his pickup at a farm protest rally and mix easily with the boys, nodding with commiseration, joking about hard times, always gently prodding a discussion toward the same profound conclusion: that a man had a God-given right to farm prosperously, that this right was being stolen away by a secret international monetary conspiracy led by the Jews and abetted by traitors in the U.S. government; and that, furthermore, the situation had reached the point where the biblical Final Days were actually at hand. The ultimate war between good and evil had begun.

Quoting the old labor-organizing song, Gordon would close the deal with the question: "Which side are you on, boys?"

Many of them said they were on his.

Gordon was born in 1920 on a North Dakota farm homesteaded since 1906 by his father, Fred—that is, on land received at low cost from federal subsidy policies. In the 1930s, many farm households in the Depression-ravaged prairies fell under the spell of radical populists and demagogues who identified international Jewry as a scapegoat for the fears and miseries of an embattled population, and accused the federal government of plotting against Americans. Like Father Coughlin, the Kahls derided President Roosevelt's economic initiatives as the "Jew Deal."

After high school, Gordon left the farm to roam the West, but like his father, he never got far away from the government largesse that he denounced others for depending on. There was a federal job in Montana as a laborer with the federal Civilian Conservation Corps, followed by a state highway work job in California, where he also picked fruit.

He spent the Second World War in the Army Air Corps as a turret gunner, flying more than fifty combat missions in the European and Pacific theaters and receiving the Purple Heart for shrapnel wounds over Germany. After his discharge, he married Joan Seil, a local farm girl. His wedding present to his wife was a 20-gauge, double-barrel shotgun.

"When Gordon returned from World War Two, he realized something was drastically wrong in the United States," Joan later told James Corcoran, recorded in his book, *Bitter Harvest.* "But he didn't know what."

He discovered his answer soon enough. For a little over a semester, he attended North Dakota Agricultural College on the GI Bill, but dropped out when he decided that the school was run by Communist sympathizers.

For a time afterward, he dallied with the Mormon church, but left when he became convinced it, too, had unsavory international connections that led to the worldwide Jewish conspiracy. During the 1950s Gordon, his wife, and children—there would eventually be six—joined the migration of the disillusioned from the Midwest to the suburbs of Los Angeles, where he found odd jobs as a car mechanic. But in the spring he always returned to the farm in North Dakota for the planting.

The 1960s were a growth era for right-wing conspiracy-theorist groups like the southern California–based John Birch Society. More influential to Kahl, however, was a far-right religious movement called Christian Identity, which would later form the philosophical bedrock of his own racist organization.

Christian Identity's theories are directly descended from Anglo-Israelism, a cult movement that sprang from Elizabethan England and peaked at the height of the British Empire. It maintains that Anglo-Saxons are descended from the ten "lost" tribes of Israel—the inhabitants driven from the northern kingdom of Solomon by the conquering Assyrians in 721 B.C. According to Anglo-Israelism, these lost tribes migrated westward to become the Saxons, who eventually conquered England. The throne of England is actually the throne of David, according to the doctrine, and on this throne Christ will literally sit on Judgment Day, after the annihilation of the children of Satan—the modern Jews.

By the 1960s, Christian Identity had adapted these theories for American consumption, asserting that the Mayflower brought the descendants of the lost tribes to America, the true promised land. In modern America, as the righteous count off the fulfillment of the prophesies—each one a mark of the beast—Armageddon would soon be fought. The site of the battle would be on the plains of Kansas or Nebraska.

This is what Gordon Kahl believed by the second half of the 1960s. Armed with such beliefs and a determination to express them, he naturally drifted into neo-Nazi and other far-right militarist cultures, including the then-moribund Ku Klux Klan. With such a basis, it was easy for him to augment his beliefs with whatever theories seemed to fit—for example, Gordon insisted that President Kennedy had been assassinated in 1963 on the orders of world Jewish leaders because Kennedy had discovered their secret plot for international domination.

Meanwhile, the wanderlust remained with him. In 1972, while working as a roustabout in the oilfields of West Texas, he flirted with fringe neo-Nazi and Klan-like groups, finally discovering Posse Comitatus in 1974. Within a year he was named its statewide coordinator.

* * *

Springing from its Christian Identity roots, Posse Comitatus had been founded in 1969 in Portland, Oregon, by Henry L. Beach, a retired dry-cleaning shop owner who belonged to an American Nazi offshoot group called the Silver Shirts, which had been popular during radical populist stirrings in the 1930s.

Posse comitatus, a Latin phrase, means, literally, the power of a county. Its basic doctrines are expressed in the organization's handbook, which stated that "a county government is the highest form of government in our Republic [and] the county sheriff is the only legal law enforcement officer in the United States." Furthermore, it says, "the sheriff is accountable and responsible only to the citizens who are the inhabitants of his county." If the sheriff fails to satisfactorily perform his duties, "the Posse Comitatus has the lawful right under natural law to act in the name of the sheriff . . ."

In other words, the Posse can take the law into its own hands, without regard to higher authority. The Posse believes that the federal government has no right to interfere in any local affairs.

Some nativist right-wing groups merely railed about the federal government. Others were militant and action-oriented, looking toward the day when a republic could be proclaimed in which only white Christian males would have legal standing. Posse members were encouraged to underscore their "individual sovereignty" by eschewing government-issued instruments such as driver's licenses. Among many members, not paying federal income taxes was viewed as an act of valor.

At the Posse's base was the belief that the United

States was founded as an exclusively Christian nation but that its Constitution, firmly rooted in the Bible, had been corrupted by an international Jewish conspiracy. To destroy America, that conspiracy had created a rapacious federal income tax at the behest of the hated Federal Reserve Board. The Posse maintained that the Fed, under secret control of eight Jewish-owned international banks since 1913, deviously manipulated interest rates to ruin the American economy and destroy Christianity, to bring about the triumph of the "Synagogue of Satan."

It was a conspiracy theory tailor-made for a man like Gordon Kahl, and for a place like the distressed American agricultural heartland of the late 1970s and the 1980s, where farmers—in debt up to their ears—were losing hope, facing ruin, and looking for reasons why. That was when Gordon Kahl came back to the heavily mortgaged farm that he had inherited from his father near Medina, North Dakota, 125 miles west of Fargo. This time, he came home with all the answers.

The FBI first began taking a serious look at the Posse in 1975, when rumors spread that members were plotting an assassination attempt against Vice President Nelson Rockefeller. By then the Posse had chapters in twenty-three states, mostly concentrated in the prairie and farm states. Posse recruiting also was picking up in the industrial Midwest, where auto workers were being laid off in droves. By the end of the decade, Posse membership was estimated at over 25,000.

At one central Posse location in Wisconsin, James Wickstrom, the group's "national director of counterinsurgency," had even founded a "township" on a wooded 570-acre compound. There, about two hundred followers lived, and trained in survivalist skills. Wickstrom's radio lectures were beamed throughout the U.S. heartland and his taped sermons were widely distributed at farm shows, state fairs, and other public events. The message was incessant and simple, according to Wickstrom: "Stinking Jew bankers" in control of the federal government were responsible for the plight of American farmers.

As the FBI warned its field offices that Posse members should be considered armed and dangerous, Gordon Kahl easily expanded on that message while working to place himself at the center of Posse Comitatus. Even before he inherited the North Dakota farm in the late seventies, Gordon had announced that he would no longer pay federal income taxes. He set up his own "church," named it the Gospel Doctrine Church of Jesus Christ, and appointed his eldest son, Yorie, as its bishop. In 1977, Gordon was convicted of tax evasion and spend eight months in prison before being released on parole, on condition that he pay his taxes. He refused to comply, setting up what would become a series of confrontations with authorities.

At the same time, he became something of a folk hero. Always an effective speaker, he was becoming as adept at radio and television as he was in small gatherings of farmers. Sensing the tenor of the times, he successfully added a big dash of tax protest theory to the existing racist and conspiratorial mixture—and farmers loved it.

The farm crisis worsened throughout the decade,

with interest payments breaking the backs of smaller farmers who had unwisely overexpanded to compete with corporate agricultural giants. At the heart of the expansion was the easy money of the era—encouraged by the government, bankers lent farmers funds readily, often without sufficient collateral. By 1983, with farm foreclosures sharply accelerating in states like North Dakota, farm suicides and other violence were becoming common phenomena. Wherever farmers gathered to talk over their woes, Posse Comitatus was there. With boundless energy, Gordon Kahl saw to that.

Gordon, Yorie, and an associate, farmer Scott Faul, drove in a pickup truck to farm rallies and farm foreclosures throughout the heartland, fanning the flames of protest. The Posse meetings they set up were often tumultuous affairs, as purely local concerns about lawsuits and contracts bumped shoulders with international conspiracy theories and calls to armed revolt and Armageddon. Gordon deftly balanced the buffeting winds of protest, preaching the Book of Revelation on one hand while passing out "legal karate kits" to use government regulations and snarl court foreclosure proceedings with the other. To this day, Posse suits against lenders on such pretexts as the federal Truth in Lending Act are still creeping their way through court systems.

Meanwhile, Posse agitators stepped up efforts to exploit the violence. In radio speeches broadcast throughout the farm states, Posse "guerrilla warfare" expert William Gale, a retired Army colonel, exhorted listeners to "cleanse the land" and start making dossiers with names, addresses, phone numbers, and car license plate numbers of Jews. FBI investigators turned up evidence of a Posse-issued "arrest warrant" that condemned to death a Kansas sheriff and his deputy who had displeased the Posse.

Gordon steadfastly refused to file federal income tax reports on his meager income, which seldom exceeded $10,000 a year. By 1983, with good reason, he believed his activities were being monitored by the federal government. In fact, the Internal Revenue Service hoped to move against him, but hadn't yet. On his organizing trips, however, Gordon maintained that in every town he and his loyal band visited, secret agents for Mossad, the Israeli intelligence service, were on hand to spy on him and anyone he came in contact with.

Back at home in North Dakota, Gordon and other Posse members were organizing a "township" modeled along the lines of Wickstrom's in Wisconsin. The group, known to be well-armed, had frequently and vociferously vowed a "struggle to the death" against all oppressors. Few tax agents or local sheriff's deputies, let alone the Israeli intelligence service, were interested in tangling lightly with such a force.

That changed on a Sunday in February of 1983, when five men were dispatched to arrest Gordon, who had an IRS lien against his farm for nonpayment of taxes and was named on a warrant for violation of parole. Kahl had finally gone too far by threatening to kill anyone who interfered with him. Dispatched to arrest the Posse leader were Marshal Kenneth Muir, a twenty-year veteran of the U.S. Marshal's office in North Dakota; Deputy Marshals Robert Cheshire, James Hopson, and Carl Wigglesworth; and Deputy Sheriff Bradley Kapp of Stutsman County.

Kapp had spotted Gordon's vehicle in the parking lot of a medical clinic in the dusty farm town of Medina, where a meeting of the planned township was under way. Aware that Muir had a warrant for Gordon, he radioed his office with word that he had spotted him. Was it time to make the arrest?

There was no great enthusiasm about any such confrontation among the law enforcement officers in the area. Not only did Kahl and his Posse have weapons and determination, they enjoyed widespread public support.

Darrell Graf, the town police chief, who had been listening to the police radio, cut in to suggest to Kapp: "This is a misdemeanor deal, it's no big thing. It's not worth creating a big problem over." Graf knew Gordon well, and firmly believed him when he said he'd never be taken alive. "If you're going to take him, you'd better have a thirty-man SWAT team," the chief warned.

Instead, the marshals decided to set up a roadblock.

The meeting, attended by dozens of local Posse members and a number of other local people, was in the town doctor's clinic on Water Street. Gordon, Yorie, and Scott Faul had arrived in mid-afternoon, toting rifles with banana clips. Yorie also had a holster with a pistol. Gordon had called the meeting to begin laying the path for the setting up of a self-contained, self-ruled, and self-sufficient community from whence to plot the end of the world. The atmosphere was one of paranoia.

As the meeting wore on, Scott Faul ducked outside for some air. He rushed back in. "We're being watched," he said.

There was discussion about agents from Mossad storming the clinic. But the lookout was only Deputy Sheriff Kapp, sitting in his green pickup a block and a half away with a pair of binoculars. He was waiting for the U.S. Marshals to come.

Driving a Dodge Ram Charger, Marshals Cheshire and Hopson, and Muir and Wigglesworth in an unmarked sedan, soon arrived in town and parked nearby. Except Muir, all of the men wore bulletproof vests.

The meeting broke up around five o'clock. Gordon, in a blue windbreaker, his usual baseball cap with farm equipment logo perched on his head, left the clinic in a Hornet driven by David Broer. Gordon's own brown station wagon followed them, driven by Yorie, with Joan Kahl in the front passenger seat. In the rear seat were Scott Faul and Vernon Wegner, a farm laborer who had been fired from a job as a small-town police chief for purchasing tear-gas grenades that he planned to give to a radical farmers' group.

On the deserted main street the marshals rendez-voused with Kapp, who climbed into the Ram Charger behind Cheshire. They set out after Gordon and his associates. Muir had gone north, meanwhile, to set up a roadblock ahead. Accompanying him in a separate vehicle was Steve Schnable, a town police officer.

At 5:40 P.M. police chief Graf happened to look out the window and see the Hornet come by on the road north out of town with Broer and Gordon, followed by the station wagon driven by Yorie—followed two minutes later by the marshals in their vehicles.

Another car came by, with a young couple in it. Graf flagged them down and warned them away from the road. "Get the hell out of here. There's going to be a shootout," he said.

Less than a mile out of town, Broer apparently became aware of the marshals' vehicles following. He stopped and made a U-turn in a driveway outside a mobile home.

Yorie pulled up beside him. "I think somebody is following us. Let's get out of here!"

But there was no time for that. The Charger with two marshals in it bounded up, lights flashing, blocking the sedan and station wagon.

Peering out a window from inside the mobile home, Wayne Reardon saw men with rifles getting out of their cars. Just then the phone in the Reardon home rang. It was the town police dispatcher. "Lock your doors! There might be a shootout."

"What the hell is this?" Scott yelled across at Yorie.

"I don't know. But I'm getting my gun!"

Yorie shouted at his mother to get down, and jumped out of the vehicle with his rifle aimed at the Charger. Faul followed, with Gordon right behind him. Now there were three armed men training weapons on the marshals in the Charger.

Cheshire, with a rifle, and Hopson, with a shotgun, tumbled out onto the ground and took cover.

"U.S. Marshals!" Cheshire yelled. "Put down your guns or we'll blow your fucking heads off!"

Gordon shouted back from his position behind a car. "Put your guns down and back off. There is no reason for anybody to get hurt over this."

From the back seat of the Charger, Kapp suggested getting out fast. But Muir was radioing for assistance from the Highway Patrol. The situation had already gotten out of control.

Faul called out, "What do you want?"

"I want *him,*" said Cheshire, pointing his rifle barrel at Gordon.

Faul backed away slowly, keeping his rifle at waist height. Then he cut across the road and dashed toward the woods beside the mobile home.

Wigglesworth pursued him, stomping through freezing muddy puddles in the woods. But Faul got away.

Meanwhile, Hopson stole up to the Hornet and approached Broer, frozen at the wheel. "We have a warrant for his arrest," Hopson said, nodding to where Gordon was crouched on the other side of his car.

"What do you guys want?" Gordon yelped again.

"All we want is you," said Hopson.

Gordon made no reply.

Muir and Schnable were edging on foot down the road from the roadblock they had set up a little ways north.

A shot rang out.

Cheshire cried, "I'm hit!" fell into the open door of the Charger, grabbed the radio mike and said, "Officer hit! Officer hit!"

There was another shot. Kapp fired, hitting Yorie in the stomach.

"I'm hit! I'm hit!" Yorie yelled to his father.

Gordon fired several rounds at Kapp, shattering the windshield. Kapp saw with astonishment that one of his fingers was blown off. Now Gordon fired up the road, hitting Schnable once. Another shot struck Muir in the chest and killed him immediately.

In a crouch, Gordon approached Schnable, still alive on the ground. "Don't shoot! I quit," the officer said.

"Give me your gun," Gordon demanded.

Quietly, Gordon took it and moved to the Charger, where he found Cheshire slumped bleeding in the front seat.

He raised his rifle and fired two bullets that blew apart Cheshire's head.

Astonishingly, at the town medical clinic where the meeting had been held, survivors of both sides of the shootout found themselves looking at each other. Gordon, his son critically wounded, brazenly approached Kapp, sitting there with his blood-soaked hand. Gordon patted his rifle.

"We could have talked this over without shooting."

"Was it worth it?" a terrified emergency technician on the scene asked Gordon.

"It was worth it to me." Gordon said.

Gordon walked out of the clinic, where the dead and wounded lay, and stole Schnable's police cruiser. He fled Medina, to become a fugitive and a martyr.

That night, Faul read a note Gordon had handed him before he drove off, emphasizing the dangers of being an enemy of the "Jewish-Masonic-Communist Synagogue of Satan."

Other Posse leaders adopted Gordon as a folk hero and eagerly spread the notion that somehow God had allowed Gordon to make monkeys out of his would-be captors in the government.

"It is the general feeling that the government has declared war on the people of this country," James Wickstrom crowed to his radio listeners in many states as news of the Medina shootout spread.

Ranting, racist letters from Gordon himself began arriving at Posse offices, and were immediately published in periodicals distributed throughout heartland Posse social networks, where the legend of Gordon Kahl was fast taking root.

As the T-shirts, bumper stickers, and radio ballads sprang up, the Posse widely presented the shootout as an aborted government attempt to set up Gordon as an example.

While on the run, Gordon wrote a sixteen-page manifesto—postmarked from Texas—depicting the shootout as an act of self-defense and calling Christian patriots to arms.

The meeting, he said, concerned the implementing of the "Third Continental Congress" to rebuild the "power and prestige" of the Constitution "and put our nation back under Christian common law." Suddenly, he said, information was received "that we were to be ambushed" on the way home.

He described encountering the two cars just north of Medina. "About this time they turned on their red lights, and I knew the attack was under way," he wrote.

". . . At the time the shot rang out, I heard Yorie

cry out 'I'm hit! I'm hit!' " Gordon wrote. He looked at the two men, he said, and "the one in the passenger side aimed at me, and I was sure then that they felt . . . the only thing to do was kill us all . . ."

After exchanging shots, and watching several of the lawmen fall, Gordon reported that he noticed the third man in time to see him "raise up to shoot at Scotty, who had run over to Yorie." Gordon said that he fired and the man fell to the ground. Then, "I saw the man who was behind the front end of the green Mercury raise up and aim at Scotty." The man took cover behind his car. "I fired, striking him and putting him out of the fight," Gordon wrote.

Gordon insisted that neither Vernon Wagner nor Dave Broer shot at anyone, and added that his wife had "nothing to do with it, other than the fact that she rode along with us" to the meeting.

He concluded: "I want the world to know that I take no pleasure in the death or injury of any of these people . . . When you come under attack by anyone, it becomes a matter of survival . . .

"I would have liked nothing better than to be left alone," he wrote. He denounced Jews and spoke of efforts to amend the Constitution to prohibit them from living in the U.S.

"We are a conquered and occupied nation; conquered and occupied by the Jews" and their allies, determined to "destroy Christianity and the white race." The coming struggle, Kahl said, was "between the people of the Kingdom of God and the Kingdom of Satan . . ."

He implored, "Let each of you who says that the Lord Jesus Christ is your personal savior sell his garment and buy a sword" to use against the "Synagogue of Satan."

He signed it, "Gordon Kahl, Christian Patriot."

After a few months of this heroic odyssey, Gordon turned up at a ranch owned by a Posse supporter in Arkansas. There he was treated as a hero by the farmer, but betrayed by the farmer's daughter, who was distressed about his agitated condition and his talk of killing more federal officers.

She called the FBI, but Gordon had moved again, this time to his final destination, a survivalist compound built like a military bunker complex into a hill near the Arkansas-Missouri border up a deep hollow of the Ozark Mountains. There, in the leafy cover, stood mobile homes and shacks, primitive residences of more than a hundred adults and children clad in combat fatigues, encamped in the belief that Doomsday was near.

Kahl had found refuge in a small house on the edge of the 225-acre compound, which was owned by a newly emerging far-right group called the Covenant of the Sword and the Arm of the Lord. The Covenant had begun billing itself as the paramilitary arm of the Christian Identity movement.

A government assault team found Gordon at the compound on June 2.

He fired on FBI agents who tried to serve the arrest warrant. While the agents took cover and secured the rest of the compound, Lawrence County Sheriff Gene Matthews stole up from the rear of the house and gained entry. As he entered the kitchen, Gordon stepped out from behind a refrigerator and began firing.

As the two men blasted away at each other, the house filled with tear gas from canisters shot through windows. The assault lasted for an hour. Finally, a smoke grenade dropped down a stove flue, ignited some diesel fuel, and the flames began licking at the floor.

Sheriff Matthews's body was dragged out of the burning house. Gordon's was later dug out of the rubble. But the Posse refused to concede the death of one of its most prominent leaders.

Donald Laverne Hollenbeck, a national Posse organizer, publicly insisted that law enforcement officials were lying and that Gordon had survived the assault.

"He is in hiding, and he is going to show up," Hollenbeck insisted on the radio.

Nevertheless, the family held a funeral. The casket with Gordon's remains was flanked by an honor guard made up of members of local American Legion posts. Gordon was eulogized as a patriot, like Patrick Henry, Nathan Hale, or George Washington. Hundreds of friends and supporters from many states crowded around to pay their last respects. The minister, Reverend Peter Dyck, noted his many disagreements with Gordon but described him as an outstanding citizen who "paid a great price" in a brave attempt "to awaken a pacifistic public to the dangers facing these great United States of America."

Avenging Gordon's death became a major goal of the Posse and its associated far-right cults like the Covenant, which later dispatched an assassination squad to hit the federal judge presiding over the trial of supporters who had helped to harbor Gordon at the Arkansas compound. (The hit squad had a highway accident en route to the judge's house and called off its mission.)

Gordon Kahl was awarded a prominent spot in the pantheon of the racist right.

An umbrella group of far-right militant organizations called Aryan Nations, adopted Kahl's call to form a self-sufficient racist state to do battle with what Kahl had called "ZOG"—the Zionist Occupation Government that was secretly running the U.S. One offshoot defined a "point system" to award credit for killing Jews and blacks. On a nationwide computer bulletin board called "Aryan Liberty Network," there appeared a list, "Know Your Enemy," that included the addresses of "traitors," prominent Jewish organizations and names and addresses of some reporters. One Kahl admirer declared that the "Satanic" U.S. government was guilty of "murdering Christians like Gordon Kahl, who you burned in Nebuchadnezzer's oven because he would not bow to your golden Babylonian God and pay your tribute to finance Israel."

The furor over Kahl resonated throughout the far right, tied as it was to the well-publicized plight of the American farmer. It encouraged and galvanized festering neo-Nazi groups, most notably a Christian Identity–based movement called the Order, which members referred to by its German name, Bruder Schweigen, the Silent Brotherhood.

On June 18, 1984, four members of the Order approached a Denver radio talk-show host, Alan Berg, outside his home. Berg was an outspoken liberal, a

Jew who had frequently argued with right-wing agitators who phoned his radio program.

The Order hit men machine-gunned him to death. Gordon Kahl would have been proud.

CHAPTER FOUR

🔥 🔥 🔥

Palace of Gold

KEITH HAM, A prematurely aging twenty-eight-year-old who looked like the missing link between the beatnik and the hippie generations, was wandering the streets of Manhattan's East Village in 1965 when he spotted the old swami. Little did Ham know it then, but his ship had finally come in.

The son of a fundamentalist preacher, Ham had managed to get a doctorate in religious studies when he drifted into Greenwich Village's eastern edge, to a neighborhood where gentrification was still a decade away. A downscale version of San Francisco's Haight district, the East Village offered cheap rents and cheaper thrills. Its weed-strewn parks and vacant lots often formed a battleground between generations of derelicts—the old boozers and the young druggies. It was a place where a frustrated rock musician without much talent could somehow see a future as a star, where a narcissistic loudmouth with half-baked opinions could imagine he was a philosopher.

Such a man was Keith Ham, already the self-styled dean of the "Mott Street Gang," a collection of street professors who listened to the radio, argued into the night, and thought they were leading a revolution.

On this fortunate day in 1965, Ham watched with some fascination as a new neighborhood character wobbled his way up the block. This was no ordinary denizen of the East Village. Approaching was a grizzled old man with a shaved head, smiling beatifically, his saffron monk's robe furling in the wind like a battle pennant.

Ham recognized the accessories of eastern mysticism because he had a roommate, a man named Wheeler, who had been flirting for years with Indian religions. Indeed, the roommate had already been singing the praises of a Hindu sect that claimed as its sacred text the glorious and ancient *Bhagavad-Gita*, the "Song of the Lord." The *Bhagavad-Gita* spun a wondrous tale of a wandering soldier en route to battle who hitches a ride with a charioteer. The driver turns out to be the sometimes playful, sometimes vengeful, Krishna, incarnation of Vishnu, the many-lived Lord of the Universe. As the hitchhiker learns the ways of Krishna, he is led, chanting and step by step, to understand the secrets of the universe and finally to achieve eternal bliss.

In fact, Ham had even accompanied his roommate on a cheap trip to India the previous summer to search for such a man, just as the Beatles had done, although with more money and greater success. And now, on teeming Houston Street, not two blocks from home, hard against the Bowery, Keith Ham encountered a monk chanting the mantra of that mysterious sect:

"Hare Krishna, Hare Krishna. Hare Rama . . ."

The swami, it turned out, had recently journeyed from his home in Vrindaban, India, to preach among the street kids then flocking into the East Village, practically in the shadow of the soon-to-be famed temple of rock, the Fillmore East theater. These were people often willing to believe in anything with a melody, and the swami found fertile ground for his message of simple love and blind devotion. Especially attractive was the traditional image of Krishna: boyish, mischievous, wise, perpetually young. Krishna was a god who played the flute and frolicked in flowers surrounded by doting, beautiful women. In short, he was a hippie's dream.

Ham struck up a conversation with the swami and followed him to his storefront headquarters. The name stenciled on the window said: Swami A.C. Bhaktivedanta Prabhupada. Inside was a curio shop where brass gimcracks, incense, books, and other accoutrements of the movement were sold, and in an adjoining room a gathering of devoted followers, all, like the swami, in saffron robes with heads shaved—even the women—all chanting in euphonious harmony: *"Hare Krishna . . ."*

Very soon, the impressionable Ham was among them. Following him to the swami's storefront were other members of the Mott Street Gang, who first showed up for cynical amusement. But in time Ham and others from the neighborhood were wearing robes and chanting along with the rest of them.

Charisma, an authoritarian bent, and a good eye

for a dollar were among the swami's chief attributes. The swami had grandiose plans to convert all of America. In time, the word of Krishna would prevail, a national movement of yoga would engulf the continent. While most of the swami's followers swooned, more level-headed ones did some mental calculations. The swami's cash registers were ringing loudly with business from the gift shop; Krishna devotees who spent their workdays panhandling all over the city were bringing home collection cans stuffed with money; new recruits were joining up every day. And the swami was an old man. He would be needing a successor one day.

After he moved into the swami's fold, adopting the new Krishna name of Kirtanananda Bhaktipada, Ham was content for a while with a simple life of chanting Krishna's name incessantly, avoiding meat, and following the path to eternal bliss by fund-raising and preaching on the sidewalks.

The swami, devoted to the spirit of the god Krishna, was evidently a holy man who practiced what he preached and lived a life of chastity, vegetarianism, and pacifism, if not self-sacrifice. But Swami Prabhupada was also a phenomenally busy man, traveling constantly between his home in India and major U.S. and urban centers to set up new communes. As the movement burgeoned, it drew into its fold not only simple believers but con men, opportunists, and street toughs intent on lying low for a while. To them, chastity and pacifism were too much to ask. They settled for vegetarianism, chanting, and, of course, raising money.

* * *

In the swami's long stretches of absence, the newly devout Kirtanananda soon emerged—by virtue of his age as well as his overbearing nature—as a kind of deputy in the growing East Village Krishna commune.

Though loyal to the old swami, Kirtanananda realized that his master's ways were conservative—"fundamentalist," as he put it. The swami had spent many years rewriting the fabled *Bhagavad-Gita,* which in its original form runs less than a hundred pages. The swami's version came in at over nine hundred pages and was retitled, with a nod to the sixties vernacular, *Bhagavad-Gita: As It Is.* It sold well, but it was incomprehensible.

Once, while accompanying the old swami on a trip to India, Kirtanananda had gingerly approached his master with suggestions about sprucing up his image for the American market, with more sophisticated advertising extolling the heroic nature of his quest, or perhaps even a television series or a movie— funded by the Krishna movement and produced by Kirtanananda himself. But it was useless. The old man just smiled, raised a hand and chanted.

"Kirtanananda decided that Swami Prabhupada was an old fart who didn't know as much as he did about marketing a new idea," one former associate later said.

Of course, Swami Prabhupada's saintly mien, that wizened and inscrutable face beaming from posters pasted up on walls all over urban America, was eminently useful in recruiting and fund-raising. Even Kirtanananda acknowledged that. But to make the movement grow to its full potential, good old American entrepreneurship was required. Competition between sects in big cities was growing. The money was pouring in. Capitalistic instincts followed close by.

Throughout the late sixties, the Krishna movement took root in U.S. cities, with its main centers of strength and recruiting in New York and Los Angeles. But Krishna communities also prospered in Britain and other countries as well. The indefatigable Swami Prabhupada named his movement the International Society for Krishna Consciousness.

In 1969 the English connection gave the Krishnas their best single publicity boost when the swami's disciple, the leader of the London sect in his absence, met and befriended George Harrison, the Beatle who had fallen under the strongest influence of eastern mysticism when the band made its famous journeys to India in the sixties. Harrison, who often said that he believed he had been a yoga in a past incarnation, agreed to produce a recording of the tuneful "Hare Krishna Mantra." Recorded at Apple Records, with Harrison and Paul McCartney joining in, the Krishna anthem became an international hit and greatly increased the number of young recruits flocking to the Krishna way of life.

Meanwhile, with the swami consumed with work tending his far-flung religious empire from his base in India, Kirtanananda decided that there was too much competition in New York. At the urging of a friend, he traveled to West Virginia and looked over an abandoned farm in the hills, about eighty-five miles below Pittsburgh, not far from the interstate highway. But it was far indeed from the disruptive influences and distractions of the big city, where law enforcement authorities had begun to pay unwanted attention to the hordes of hippie and religious-cult panhandlers and solicitors—and more importantly, where "deprogrammers" working to reclaim cult members on behalf of distraught parents had started to cause serious problems for Krishna recruitment activities.

Kirtanananda, aware of the importance of both Prabhupada's image and his continuing goodwill, excitedly told the swami that he and his adherents from New York would move to West Virginia and build a new rural community there in his honor. The community would also be available to the swami as his home away from home, Kirtanananda explained. The swami, weary of big cities, blessed the idea.

It was an huge undertaking, building a working commune and a suitably opulent headquarters in the hardscrabble farmland in an alien environment. Kirtanananda and more than a hundred Krishnas from New York moved down, naming their dreamed-of earthly paradise New Vrindaban, after the sacred Indian village where the youthful Krishna was said to have performed his epic deeds, subjugating river serpents in splendid raiment while dancing with milkmaids and vanquishing enemies.

In Krishna communities elsewhere in the U.S. and abroad, Kirtanananda's counterparts—the Prabhupada disciples who headed the various individual sects and had become known as the "gurus"—chuckled at the audacity of their New York colleague. "Empire-building," one said. As it turned out, he was right.

* * *

Kirtanananda and his followers settled in for their first winter on the sprawling farmland along a mountain ridge in West Virginia's impoverished northern panhandle. The site was in the outskirts of a town named Moundsville, population 12,000. As the oddly dressed religious devotees moved in, neighboring farmers watched with some bemusement. It was, however, an area where Appalachian hospitality is a basic value, and during that first winter, neighbors generously assisted the new arrivals, donating food, helping with construction of cabins and sheds, offering advice when the spring came on keeping livestock and raising crops.

With the arrival of the glorious mountain spring, flocks of new devotees found their way down to New Vrindaban, drawn by Krishna recruiters still aggressively at work in the streets of New York, Philadelphia, and Washington, D.C. By the scores they came, in vans and pickups, as hitchhikers and bus passengers—teenagers, young couples with tiny children, single men. All had shaved heads and wore robes. And in a very short time the daily routine of Moundsville and surrounding communities was changed by their presence. Areas that had never known panhandlers now were teeming with them. In a place where people minded their own business, Krishnas even began soliciting door-to-door. There were reports that they had stepped up recruiting among local high school kids.

This, coupled with the fact that the Krishna community generated money and even a few menial jobs in an area where unemployment often reached 25 percent, created a basic conflict in attitudes toward the new neighbors in their rapidly expanding commune. On the one hand, the Krishnas had money. Most astounding to neighbors was the amount of money the Krishnas apparently were prepared to spend to buy land. Heads shook in amazement at the prices the Krishnas paid farmers for adjoining acres of land—prices five and ten times what any sensible buyer would have had to offer to get it. Very rapidly the Krishna spread expanded. In a little over a decade, New Vrindaban's original hundred acres of rolling fields with a few shacks that had neither running water nor electricity would grow to over 2,800 acres, with modern buildings and, ultimately, a palace of gold.

On the other hand, as their presence grew, the Krishnas raised concerns among many neighbors, who brought back rumors of child abuse and weapons accumulation, even of sexual wantonness at the Krishna paradise. In a fairly short time the word "cult" was being applied to the new neighbors.

One local resident told a reporter that the Krishnas, once welcomed, had come to be regarded as "no-good, tax-exempt vermin."

Inside the prospering New Vrindaban compound, Kirtanananda ingeniously manipulated the outside suspicion, and occasional hostility, into the cult leader's chief weapon: a sense among his followers that they were under siege by unseen enemies. The neighbors, Kirtanananda scoffed, were "rednecks and materialists who resent our spiritualism."

Like most Krishna communities, at New Vrindaban most devotees worked sixteen-hour days at panhandling or menial jobs and were expected to blindly follow the swami's dictates. Married couples, whose partners often were chosen arbitrarily by Kirtanananda, were usually restricted to sexual relations once a month. Children were removed from their parents at an early age and segregated in dormitories.

Paranoia flowered. In 1973 it was fertilized by reality when several local men attacked New Vrindaban at gunpoint, to "rescue" a fifteen-year-old daughter who had been recruited into the cult. The assailants shot up the place, but no one was hurt. However, Kirtanananda seized on the incident as a rallying cry. Soon, in the telling, the relatively small incident became a major armed assault on the Krishna compound by wild-eyed bikers, while the local police looked the other way.

In great alarm, Kirtanananda wrote to Prabhupada in India to tell him of the battle, which he now likened to the opening skirmishes of Armageddon.

"Why are you not keeping guns?" the swami wrote back, according to reporters John Hubner and Lindsey Gruson in their book, *Monkey on a Stick: Murder, Madness and the Hare Krishnas*. "We are not followers of Gandhi's philosophy."

Into New Vrindaban from the hard city streets poured a new breed of Krishna devotee: young men with records of violent crime, with a familiarity with guns and a readiness to use them. Soon, an armed "defense force" patrolled the grounds to enforce rules, under the guise of providing protection from hostile outsiders. Quietly, stockpiles of weapons and ammunition built up.

The isolation intensified with the fear that the outside world was poised to attack.

In his preaching, some followers who fled in alarm would later say, Kirtanananda began to sound less an exponent of Hindu mysticism than a paranoid religious fanatic. Perhaps inevitably, the joyous *Bhagavad-Gita* as Kirtanananda interpreted it began to sound more like the grim, apocalyptic Book of Revelation.

By the mid-1970s the community at New Vrindaban numbered about five hundred people. As old age slowed him down, Pradhupada's visits became less frequent. Increasingly regarding himself as the swami's logical successor at the head of the international movement, Kirtanananda became more autocratic, enforcing codes on what could be discussed and when, arbitrarily choosing marital partners, and separating children from their parents in locked dormitories.

Prabhupada died in India in 1977, at the age of eighty-one. At the master's death, the International Society of Krishna Consciousness claimed adherents in temples all over the world, but chiefly in the U.S. On his deathbed, Prabhupada had designated eleven new "gurus," regional swamis who would be responsible collectively for running the international movement in its blissful endeavors once he was gone. Ruling the East Coast Krishna kingdom from his bastion in West Virginia, Kirtanananda, of course, was one of the eleven.

"He thought he was leaving the movement to eleven bishops," one former follower said. "What he really did was create eleven competing popes."

A power struggle was inevitable. Kirtanananda—heading the richest and most influential of the Krishna communities, building an earthly paradise in the hills of West Virginia—vowed to win it. Other gurus, Kirtanananda declared, were "in *maya*"—living lives of sin.

At the base of his power was an impressive flow of money. From 1981 to 1985, federal prosecutors would later claim, Krishna devotees based at New Vrindaban generated $10.5 million just from street sales in various cities of counterfeit caps, T-shirts, and bumper stickers bearing trademark characters from "Peanuts" and other comic strips.

The first major public sign of trouble in the Krishna empire had come a few years after Prabhupada's death, when a Krishna sect in California was implicated in charges of drug-money laundering. Its leader, Alexander Kulik, was convicted in 1979 of heroin distribution.

But in West Virginia all still looked rosy, as devotees worked day and night to complete New Vrindaban's greatest monument. In 1980, Kirtanananda dedicated New Vrindaban's crowning glory, the spectacular, Ozlike Palace of Gold, an ornate domed temple to Krishna that stood on an Appalachian foothill, its roof gleaming with a layer of 22-carat gold leaf, its walls sheathed in two hundred tons of marble inlaid with Italian onyx. Inside the temple, whose chambers were adorned with fine wood fittings and gold scrollwork, soft colors glowed through intricately designed stained-glass windows, bathing bronze statues of Hindu gods and paintings depicting the life of the Lord Krishna. In one central chamber stood a great statue of Prabhupada himself. Interestingly, it was cast not in bronze, but in wax.

The grounds were landscaped to slope gracefully

down from the palace in cascades of roses—more than three thousand bushes in all—bordered with well-tended mazes and splashing fountains. At the base of the hill was a man-made lake where a gold-and-white swan boat provided rides for the tourists who had started arriving by the busload, drawn by advertisements the Krishnas had placed around the country.

It was an amazing monument to faith and to one man's will, constructed over the years by the hands of hundreds of devotees, who did the work using do-it-yourself manuals bought in hardware stores. Visitors drawn to the site paid their four-dollar admission, roamed the grounds, flocked to the restaurant and the gift shops where Krishna goods were sold, snapping pictures of the idyllic scene and the chanting, saffron-robed devotees who never seemed to lose their energy for devotion. Soon, the Palace of Gold was a major tourist attraction in the region, generating more than 200,000 visitors and millions of dollars a year. The *New York Times* Sunday travel section called it "West Virginia's Taj Mahal."

Never one to miss an opportunity for favorable publicity, Swami Kirtanananda exulted to reporters, "This is a Krishnaland, for devotion of the spirit."

By now the hardy band of devotees who had built New Vrindaban out of the hard-luck farmland of the West Virginia hills had grown to over seven hundred in number. They lived, outwardly, in simple devotion, chanting, dancing, meditating, and working the land. Visitors had no inkling of the authoritarian nature of the commune. The guns and other weapons stayed out of sight when strangers were around. So did the guards, who dressed not in monks' robes, but in camouflage military fatigues and enforced the rules.

The first bloody incident involved Charles St. Denis, who used the name Chakradara. St. Denis was a cocaine dealer living on Krishna land, where he ran a garden nursery business, with 50 percent of the official gardening profits going to his master, Kirtanananda, down the road at New Vrindaban.

St. Denis was a garrulous, hefty 250-pounder with a seventeen-inch neck and a prodigious taste for booze and drugs. He was a burned-out hippie and LSD fanatic whose ambition to find religion as a full-fledged Krishna and join the commune down the road was in constant conflict with his determination to have a good time and answer to no one but himself. This formed a critical dilemma for St. Denis, who tried to have it both ways—he wanted the impossible: *Animal House* with serenity.

He died when he thought he was going to a party.

In June of 1983, St. Denis accepted an invitation to a party from a Krishna friend, Daniel Reid—even though he knew well that Reid had been publicly accusing him all over New Vrindaban of raping his wife. Thinking his denial was sufficient, and utterly unconcerned about a real-estate dispute he had recently been involved in with several other Krishnas, St. Denis happily drove to a shack on one of the New Vrindaban hills where Reid had told him the party was.

It turned out to be a party of three—St. Denis and the two Krishnas who were waiting for him when he arrived, Reid and Thomas Drescher, the much feared chief enforcer of New Vrindaban.

Drescher, who went by the name Tirtha, was a pistol-packing goon who thought that St. Denis's nursery business was encroaching on some mountain property he himself owned. A combat veteran, Drescher led the cadre of Krishnas who maintained the commune's arsenal of weapons and patrolled the community in camouflage uniforms to root out signs of dissent and betrayal.

"Hare Krishna," St. Denis said when he opened the door of the cabin and saw the other two men.

"Chant," Drescher ordered, pulling the trigger.

St. Denis was shot twelve times. When he kept moaning, refusing to die, they stabbed him in the chest and then finished him off using a hammer to drive a screwdriver into his brain. They buried him in a muddy three-foot-deep grave they had prepared on New Vrindaban land.

It was another devotee, Steve Bryant, who brought the rumors into the open—and paid for his treachery with his life.

At the time, the best estimates were that there were about 10,000 full-time adherents of various Hare Krishna sects, about half of them in the U.S., where they were most visible panhandling, proselytizing, and selling merchandise in airports and other public places.

A lifelong gun nut and member of the fanatic John Birch Society, Bryant was living miserably with his wife Jane and their young son in the London Krishna community in the late 1970s. There, Steve had a menial job in a Krishna incense factory.

He had heard about the spectacular activities at New Vrindaban, and shortly after the Palace of Gold was dedicated, he moved to West Virginia with his wife and son to join the energetic Kirtanananda. At New Vrindaban, Bryant made it his mission to get Kirtanananda's attention with much talk of grandiose money-raising schemes. At one point Kirtanananda suggested that Bryant would become the manager of the New Vrindaban resort hotel, which was under construction near the Palace of Gold.

Bryant did not get the job. Unwisely, Kirtanananda had made an enemy, a disgruntled job-seeker.

In 1984, Bryant finally left New Vrindaban in a rage after returning from a Krishna recruiting trip and finding that his wife no longer shared his bed. Bryant believed that Kirtanananda had brainwashed his wife Jane to divorce him and to stay behind in New Vrindaban, where he had bestowed her and their two sons—Sarva and Nimai—like a present to another husband.

Bryant began condemning New Vrindaban to anyone who would listen, voicing his disgust at the growing Disneylandlike atmosphere, where money was all that mattered. After he left, Bryant returned one morning and tried to take his little boys with him. But he didn't get far with them. Two van loads of New Vrindaban armed defense forces gave chase, cornering him at a suburban shopping center. They forcibly took the boys back. Obsessed, Bryant spent nearly a year roaming the country to spread the word that Kirtanananda was a fraud.

In his agitating, Bryant found a receptive audience in other Krishna communities, partly because of jealousy over Kirtanananda's spectacular achievements,

and partly because refugees from the abuses at New
Vrindaban had formed a network of exiles throughout the country. Along with Bryant, they maintained
that Kirtanananda and other gurus appointed by
Prabhupada had betrayed Krishna principles.

Bryant was vociferous in his charges against
Kirtanananda. He traveled the country railing
against Kirtanananda in his beat-up van, distributing
his charges in a lengthy expose that he had typed and
photocopied, which he titled *The Guru Business,* and
an abridged version of the same, *Jonestown in
Moundsville.* Bryant summarized allegations that had
come to swirl around New Vrindaban in dissident
circles of autocratic rule, weapons stockpiling, and
drug trafficking.

Bryant's obsessions had gone beyond allegations,
to a plan. He told fellow dissidents that he was hoping to kill Kirtanananda and the other "bogus gurus"
himself. He insisted that Krishna himself had called
upon him to do so.

In the late summer of 1985, Bryant made a desperate foray back to Marshall County, West Virginia,
the location of New Vrindaban, where he notified
the local sheriff of his charges and discussed the like-
lihood of a holy war at New Vrindaban. He asked for
and got protective custody in the county jail, where
he went on at great length, but failed to give the wary
cops what they really needed, which was names,
dates, places: evidence.

"Steve told all kinds of incredible stories about
what was going on up there," the sheriff, Donald
Bordenkircher, said. I kept saying, 'Steve, you've got
to substantiate it. Give us names.' "

Bryant told the sheriff he couldn't do that because people were afraid for their lives. Suspecting that Bryant was merely a lunatic with frustrated ambitions, the cops threw him out of the jail and sent him on his way. Bryant got into his van and roamed as usual.

Back in West Virginia, paranoia was aided by reality.

About six weeks after Bryant left the area, Kirtanananda was attacked without warning at the Palace of Gold by a wild-eyed new devotee. The assailant whacked the swami across the head with a steel pole, sending him into a coma from which he barely recovered. Weeks later, feeble, suffering fainting spells, unable to walk without a cane, Kirtanananda called a press conference. With menacing-looking guard dogs on each side of him, the swami charged that Steve Bryant's calumnies had motivated the attacker.

While there was no evidence of direct collusion, the swami may have had a point. Sentenced to fifteen months in jail for the assault, Kirtanananda's attacker received an unsigned letter from Berkeley, California—where Bryant was known to be staying—assuring him that he would be "spiritually rewarded for attacking Swami Kirtanananda."

Retribution soon followed.

On May 22, 1986, the thirty-six-year-old Bryant had come to the end of his road. He was weary of roaming the country in his ten-year-old Dodge van, preaching his Jeremiad to Krishna followers and anyone else who would listen. New Vrindaban was,

Bryant maintained, a pasteboard kingdom crowned by a Palace of Gold. The famed Palace of Gold, he and other dissidents maintained, had been financed not by women and children begging on the streets, as Kirtanananda liked to say, but by money from product counterfeiting.

Even now, he said, hit men were in pursuit of him.

In the predawn hours of May 22, 1986, Bryant had parked the van on a lonely street in West Los Angeles. He began his ritual chant. He did not see the other vehicle slide into the shadows of the street, and he did not see the New Vrindaban assassin creep up to the van while he chanted:

"Hare Krishna, Hare Krishna . . ."

The police found Bryant slumped over the steering wheel, dead of two bullets fired into his head point-blank with a .45.

Bryant's death, coming as it did after he had told police that someone from New Vrindaban was out to kill him, brought to life ongoing criminal investigations by the FBI, the IRS, and local and county law enforcement agencies in West Virginia. In all, thirty active and former members of the New Vrindaban commune were subpoenaed for testimony.

As word crackled through the Krishna communities that Bryant had been murdered, it was whispered that he was meant to be seen as a "Monkey on a stick," an allusion to a practice in India where banana plantation owners discourage monkeys from raiding banana groves by impaling a monkey on a stake as an example.

Within months Drescher was charged with the

murder of Bryant, which law enforcement authorities maintained he had done under orders. Drescher also was charged in the St. Denis murder. He was convicted of both.

With active criminal investigations intensifying, Kirtanananda professed to be unfazed by the allegations made by people like Bryant, which he dismissed as "absurd." His West Virginia community was by far the largest and most famous in the Hare Krishna empire, he noted: It stood to reason that other swamis at less-prosperous Krishna communities were jealous, and using people like Bryant to spread lies.

In May of 1990, after a two-year inquiry, a federal grand jury in West Virginia indicted Kirtanananda and two followers with three counts of racketeering, one count of conspiracy to commit murder, and six counts of mail fraud. Among the charges was that Kirtanananda had taken part in a conspiracy to murder Bryant.

A year later, Kirtanananda was sentenced to thirty years in prison after being convicted of racketeering as well as mail fraud. He was not convicted on the charge of conspiring to murder Bryant.

A federal appeals court later ruled that Kirtanananda should have a new trial because some of the evidence introduced at the first trial about the sexual molestation of children and abuse of women at New Vrindaban was prejudicial and should not have been admitted. That new trial was set for late in 1994.

CHAPTER FIVE

Come and Get Us!

FOR DAYS, FORENSIC technicians worked grimly to piece together the remains scooped out of the rubble of a neighborhood in West Philadelphia that had been burned down by police serving a final eviction notice in 1985 on a cult that called itself Move.

The bones were sorted by size and whatever other little could be found: big or small, male or female, adult or child. When the pieces were finally assembled into skeletons, the body count was made. There were eleven dead in all.

The children were supposed to be the future of Move, which called itself a back-to-nature group, even though its members stubbornly insisted on living in a crowded city neighborhood, where they instigated complicated confrontations with neighbors and police.

The children would be the pure generation, raised on raw foods, unsullied by modern education, protected within the commune from the oppression of the world.

Five of the bodies were children. The youngest, a girl of six, had never known any life but this.

In May of 1985, Philadelphia authorities clumsily ended a frustrating standoff with the cult by dropping a bomb on a rooftop, killing all Move members inside a house and starting a fire that destroyed a city neighborhood. And it had not been the first standoff with Move that ended in tragedy.

Through it all, Move remained maddeningly impervious to the application of logic. And that was perhaps the greatest tragedy of all. No one ever really understood that they believed in nothing more than defiance to the death.

Move's founder was a middle-aged black man, Vincent Leaphart, a grade-school dropout, one of ten children raised in West Philadelphia by parents who had migrated to the city from the south in the 1920s. But Leaphart had a most unlikely partner in the endeavor: Donald J. Glassey, a white man in his middle twenties, a product of the comfortable suburbs who was teaching classes at Penn while completing a master's degree in social work and, as he would later say, "looking to make the world a better place." The two met at a fair-housing protest in the early 1970s and discovered that they had many things in common.

Their alliance was forged at a propitious time, in the racially mixed neighborhood called Powelton Village, an area of run-down Victorian homes, side-by-side row homes, and rooming houses in West Philadelphia bordering the campuses of the University of Pennsylvania and Drexel University. Along with the college population drawn by the cheap rents, the neighborhood attracted young professionals busily fixing up the rambling old houses, as well as a collection of disaffiliated street preachers, aging hippies, and simple drifters.

Leaphart, who had an extensive arrest record, including time served for armed robbery and car theft, had been scratching out a living in rapidly gentrifying Powelton Village as a handyman and dog-walker. But what he did best was talk—at length, and to anyone who would listen—about the injustices of what he denounced as the "System."

Leaphart's firebrand black-radical intensity impressed Glassey at a time when liberal reformers such as himself also felt under siege in Philadelphia, a blue-collar city whose African-American population had long bristled with racial grievances, many directed at the police. In 1972, Philadelphia had just elected a new mayor, Frank Rizzo, a barrel-chested, reactionary former police commissioner known for both braggadocio and ruthlessness. Rizzo, who once vowed to "make Attila the Hun look like a faggot," was widely reviled among blacks and white liberals, who remembered him as the street cop who delighted in raiding coffeehouses to root out "subversives." As police chief, Rizzo had once humiliated a group of Black Panthers by ordering them to strip as their girlfriends looked on and news photographers snapped pictures.

By the time he met Glassey, Leaphart—who wore his hair in tangled Rastafarian dreadlocks—had already attracted a small assembly of followers. Glassey added academic cachet to the mix. Besides a surfeit of idealism and a pedantic readiness to explain complex political theories, Glassey had another virtue that the calculating Leaphart found quite enticing. Glassey owned half of a huge, decaying old Gothic house at 307 North 33rd street—a house with room enough for a crowd. In 1973, Leaphart moved in with his menagerie—more than thirty mangy dogs and cats—and a band of followers: five males, three females, two of them Leaphart's sisters, and their small children. The small commune called itself the American Christian Movement for Life—Move, for short.

Assuming a role as head of the commune, Leaphart changed his name to John Africa. Except for Glassey, the followers all took the same surname, Africa. Glassey, meanwhile, went to work immortalizing John Africa, telling him, "You have some fascinating ideas here. You should write them down."

Leaphart could barely read or write, but he certainly could talk. For nearly a year, as Leaphart rambled on, devising a convoluted philosophy, Glassey dutifully typed away. The result was a 300-page manifesto titled "The Teachings of John Africa" and later retitled simply "The Book." It was Move's bible —a bewildering compendium of nostrums about healthy living based on a return to nature, laced with conspiracy theories—among them that street drugs were a government plot to subjugate blacks—as well as detailed lessons on disparate subjects such as veterinary care, the tyranny of science, breast feeding, and the inevitability of confrontation with the System.

Gradually, the house filled up with more followers of John Africa—by 1975 about thirty-five people were jammed into the household: adults and children, male and female, including a number of ex-cons and drug addicts. All of the adults were united in hatred of the "System." And all were blindly obedient to the often whimsical dictates of John Africa, which were enforced by a small cadre of his top aides who had assumed grandiose titles such as Defense Minister and Minister of Information. Group unity was instilled in nightly meetings, during which the leader would expound passionately. "It was like he communicated with life itself," one of the early Move followers would later recall.

Women were expected to procreate and raise the next generation of pure Move soldiers. When a woman gave birth, she was required to sever the umbilical cord with her own teeth and then lick the baby clean. Dissent was unheard of. Physical fitness was ensured in daily exercise meetings, when as many as three hundred pushups were required. Though a rigid dietary regime centered on uncooked food, and vegetables were mandatory, John Africa occasionally rewarded the faithful with "distortion days," when they could binge all day on take-out junk food.

Meanwhile, as its numbers grew, Move's community activism intensified. Members skillfully sought news media attention. For years Move seemed to be everywhere with its vociferous presence, screaming threats through ever-present bullhorns at political and protest rallies, picketing a baffling array of events and institutions, from the city zoo to local hospitals, colleges, and even veterinary clinics.

Given this public militancy, confrontations with neighbors and with police became commonplace. Denouncing police brutality, Move members were frequently hauled into court on various misdemeanor or civil complaints, most of them having to do with public nuisance, sanitation, and zoning violations. In one seven-month period ending in 1974, Move members were arrested a total of 150 times. Move defendants always represented themselves in court, with their colleagues in rowdy attendance, raising constant objections and shouting denunciations of the System. These spectacles drew even more media attention, as court sessions dissolved in comic chaos with judges often reduced to frustrated sputtering. No one had ever seen anything like it. Judges, lawyers, cops, and reporters alike were dumbfounded by the ranting and raving, unkempt and unwashed, screaming band of wild-haired, foul-smelling revolutionaries who appeared to have no discernible political goal other than pure confrontation in a particularly bizarre form of street theater.

A reporter for the *Philadelphia Inquirer* marveled at Move's antics when the group protested at a 1974 meeting of governors of the thirteen original states in a downtown restaurant. "It was this night that Move members demonstrated their most baffling ability: How can they talk continuously, punctuating each phrase with an obscenity, without ever saying anything comprehensible?"

In time Glassey himself became disillusioned enough to split with John Africa. He moved out, telling friends that he was worried about the growing talk of violence. "He wanted absolute control over everyone," Glassey said of John Africa.

By then the Move house had become a civic nuisance that strained even the liberal tolerance of Powelton Village. Neighbors regularly called the cops about the Move dogs, cats, and other animals roaming freely; the junk, garbage, and human waste tossed out of windows; the naked toddlers wandering around unsupervised; the racket and the threats. As the group's notoriety grew, Move erected a stockade fence around the house and built a plank stage out front. They set up loudspeakers and used them day and night to bellow invectives and issue challenges to the police. Goading wary police surveillance officers who frequented the site, they even bragged about acquiring the means to build an atomic bomb.

At the nightly meetings, John Africa exhorted followers to prepare for a showdown with police. In the winter of 1976, Move upped the ante. After a scuffle between Move members and police, Move's loudspeakers suddenly boomed with the charge that club-wielding cops had stormed into the house during the melee and killed one of their infants, a six-month-old baby named Life Africa.

After police furiously denied the charge as ridiculous, two city councilmen, along with a community activist and a newspaper reporter and photographer, were invited into the Move house, served a ritualistic dinner, and then escorted to a dimly lighted upstairs room. They gasped at what they were shown: a dead infant decomposing on a bed of dirt and garbage inside a cardboard box. A former member, Valerie Janet Brown, later confirmed that the baby had died of natural causes in a commune where modern medicine was prohibited. Move used the death "for propaganda purposes," she told a reporter years later.

The publicity had its intended effect, keeping Move in the headlines. Move's stridency was soon echoed by a loud clamor from its long-suffering neighbors, who demanded that the city do something about blatant zoning, health, fire, and other licensing violations as the Move house grew louder. In May of 1977, when the city obtained an order to evict a Move member from a nearby building, a half-dozen Move members wearing army fatigues appeared on the stage of their headquarters brandishing shotguns, rifles, handguns, and clubs to protest. Their loudspeaker blared with a demand for the release of all Move members then in jail. Otherwise, no one was coming in. "The only way you will come in is over our dead bodies," the loudspeaker boomed.

Police began round-the-clock surveillance of the compound. The next month, as authorities intensified their investigation, Donald Glassey himself was arrested and charged with possession of marijuana as well as falsifying information on federal firearms forms. In exchange for a reduced sentence and a place in the Federal Witness Protection Program, Glassey agreed to become an informant against Move. His work led to the discovery of a cache of Move armaments—including time bombs and pipe bombs—in cars near the house. Federal weapons charges were added to those against John Africa. Unknown to police, however, John Africa managed to slip out of the compound and flee.

As the defiance continued, Mayor Rizzo finally had had enough. "Move," he growled ominously, "has had its day. They're going to be removed from the community for a long time."

As it turned out, like most other vows the blustery mayor would make, this would be a lot easier said than done.

* * *

The standoff became a full-fledged blockade in March of 1978, when Rizzo ordered a large force of police to surround the house. Whatever his faults, however, the mayor was a skillful police tactician, and negotiations for a surrender continued for months. But in early August, calling Move "a bunch of complete idiots," Mayor Rizzo said that time had run out. Plans were made to storm the house.

Delbert Orr Africa, a cocky and street-smart young black man who seemed to take special delight in goading the cops, declared that this was fine with Move. He broadcast a response guaranteed to infuriate the mayor: "We're not giving up. Rizzo's going to get his fat face punched all over the fucking United States as the killer of black women and children."

Rizzo made his move on August 8. Just before dawn, three hundred flak-jacketed cops and firemen, covered by sharpshooters in windows of nearby houses, moved toward the ramshackle Move headquarters. As hundreds of spectators strained against barricades blocks away, Move's floodlights and loudspeakers snapped to life.

"If you want us out, you'll have to bring us out dead!"

Police Inspector George Fencl, who had been directing the blockade, raised a bullhorn to his lips.

"You have exactly two minutes in which to come out."

"The gate's open!" Move crowed.

Fencl passed the bullhorn to a priest, who implored, "I plead with you, let the children come out . . . No one is going to get hurt. Let me come in and I'll walk out with you."

"Fuck you, priest!"

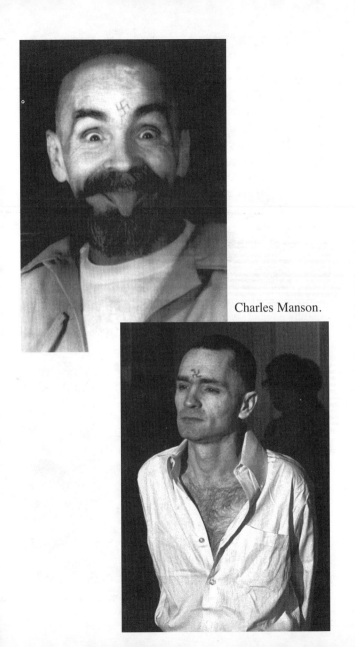

Charles Manson.

The Reverend Jim Jones preaching with clenched fist at unknown location. (UPI/BETTMANN)

Death reigned in the meeting hall of Jim Jones's People's Temple. (AP/WIDE WORLD PHOTOS)

Gordon W. Kahl of the Posse Comitatus. (AP/WIDE WORLD PHOTOS)

Vincent Leaphart, known also as John Africa, founded the radical MOVE organization. (AP/WIDE WORLD PHOTOS)

Alleged religious cult leader Jeffrey Lundgren is taken into court in Plainsville, Ohio. (AP/WIDE WORLD PHOTOS)

Texas Attorney General Jim Mattox (white shirt, center) views cauldron of bones from a ritual held by El Padrino. (UPI/BETTMANN)

Hare Krishna leader Kirtanananda Swami Bhaktipada. (UPI/BETTMANN)

Luc Jouret, founder of the Order of the Solar Temple.
(AP/WIDE WORLD PHOTOS)

Move members filed silently into place onto the stage and took up a chant, "Baby killers! Baby killers!"

At 6:30 a small group of cops rushed the side of the house with a battering ram, smashing through a window. Rats streamed out.

"Any force will be met with force!" Move's loudspeaker boomed.

Within minutes two dozen cops in battle gear were over the wall and inside the compound. But they held their positions as cannon blasts of water from fire-truck snorkles were drilled at the house, flooding the basement.

At 8:15, with Move still stubbornly dug in, gunshots rang out from the house. Police responded in force. For two minutes the air was thick with furious gunfire.

A cop crouching in the yard heard someone shout out a window, "Come on in! But call home first and make sure your insurance policy is paid up." Other cops claimed to have seen Move members holding small children and babies in front of them as shields.

The cops were in the house in raging fury now, and further resistance was impossible. On the street, police officer James J. Ramp, fifty-two, lay dead of a rifle wound. Three other cops and four firemen were wounded.

Mayor Rizzo, nearly apoplectic that a cop had been killed and others wounded by Move, ordered that the house be torn down. That afternoon, city workers bulldozed it into a mound of rubble. Nine of the Move cultists would subsequently receive life sentences for the shootout.

Philadelphians breathed a collective sigh of relief, thinking they had heard the last of Move.

So it was with a startled sense of déjà vu that city residents learned a few years later that another Move house was in full operation, this time with a military-like bunker on the roof.

The new location was at 6221 Osage Avenue in West Philadelphia, a working-class black neighborhood of well-tended row homes in neat lines of blocks just off the expanse of a park called Cobbs Creek.

In many ways, the coming confrontation would resemble the one of 1978. But this time the death count would be higher, and the city would never live down how it ended.

In the years after the 1978 shootout, Move members who weren't arrested had scattered, some to an affiliate chapter in Richmond, Virginia; others to a house in Rochester, New York, where John Africa soon reappeared. A force of federal and local cops stormed that house in 1981 and successfully arrested him on the outstanding fugitive weapons charges. He was subsequently acquitted of the charges, however, and again dropped out of sight.

That was the same year that his followers began gathering again back in Philadelphia, in a row house in the middle of the block on Osage Avenue owned by Louise James, a sister of John Africa, who would herself leave the group in fear within a year.

At first, only women and children moved in. Some of the children were those of Move members imprisoned after the 1978 shootout. But gradually, male Move members drifted in. With them came the usual collection of cats and dogs, followed by the usual complaints from neighbors: filth, noise, harassment, and threats to anyone who raised an objection to the disruption of the neighborhood's normal serenity. Loudspeakers went up; the all-night harangues began.

The situation deteriorated further in 1984, when Move began working on additions and interior alterations to the house. Neighborhood alarm intensified when the cultists nailed boards over the windows and began building a bunker on the roof.

Rizzo was long out of office. Philadelphia now had its first black mayor, Wilson Goode, a soft-spoken son of rural sharecroppers, a respected former city administrator who watched the Move build-up with a gnawing sense of apprehension as city officials tried to find a way to deal with the mounting complaints against the cult.

In April, a large force of police rushed to the scene when a Move member identified as Frank James Africa, twenty-six years old, appeared on the roof brandishing a shotgun. But he quickly disappeared back inside. A very long standoff had begun.

Throughout the summer, as police stood by, Move members strutted on the platform outside the house. "Come August eighth, we will take care of you people!" they taunted. August 8, as city and police officials well knew, was the anniversary of the Powelton Village shootout.

When August 8 arrived, the scene on Osage Avenue bore an eerie resemblance to the one in Powelton Village six years earlier. At dawn, three hundred cops and firefighters assembled in battle gear in a bivouac area near the park. Move's loudspeakers blasted away, but the battle remained rhetorical. The cops didn't make a move.

A violent confrontation appeared inevitable, and the last thing Mayor Goode wanted was to preside over another Move shootout.

In fact, he would preside over something worse.

For months police officials debated how to storm the house if it became necessary. In command of the tactical planning was the city managing director, Leo Brooks, a retired Army two-star general. As police officials argued over tactics, Brooks pointed out a basic problem: Annoying as it was, Move had not committed an overt criminal act. Building a bunker on a roof was perhaps a zoning violation, one of many—but hardly cause for storming the house in force. Others argued history that showed that the longer they waited, the more likely the outcome would be violent. Police did have outstanding arrest warrants for two men known to be in the house, but serving them with the risk of bloodshed—with children in the house—was another matter altogether.

Still, with a former general running things, the planning began to take on the feeling of a military campaign, and indeed it was given a military-type code name, "Operation Move." Aerial surveillance had spotted a trapdoor opening onto the Move roof behind the bunker—meaning the cultists could quickly get into a good strategic position if police decided to storm the house. Initially, the plan under discussion centered around the idea of using high-powered water cannons, capable of shooting 1,000 gallons a minute, to blast away at the plywood bunker and demolish it. However, an alternate plan also was under discussion. It was predicated on a much different approach: The police department's bomb squad said that it could scale the roof and place a tear-gas generator at the mouth of the trapdoor to force the residents out onto the street.

Inside the house, Move quietly prepared for the final confrontation. Again the loudspeaker told the cops to come and get them.

Neighborhood pressure increased throughout 1985 as residents—people proud of their homes in a safe, decent neighborhood—complained that the danger at the Move house had become obvious. At least three neighbors reported that they had been assaulted by Move members. Some threatened to get guns and take matters in their own hands if police refused to act.

In April neighbors reported that armed men were seen inside the twelve-by-twelve-foot rooftop bunker, which had now been reinforced. For months, police surveillance officers had watched Move members hauling out boxfuls of dirt, which were placed neatly at the curb for removal by the city Sanitation Department. Neighbors had seen the same thing, and rumors swept Osage Avenue: Move had dug underground tunnels to wire the block and blow it up. In fact, Move was excavating the cellar of the house to use as a bunker.

Responding to the furor, Mayor Goode announced that the police had no "legal basis" to make arrests simply to "remove the problem from the neighborhood." An editorial in the tabloid *Philadelphia Daily News,* summing up popular reaction to Goode's recalcitrance, demanded action.

The police stepped up their preparations, still worried about the difficulties of placing a tear-gas dispenser on the roof. A key figure in the planning, Lieutenant Frank Powell, the supervisor of the bomb disposal unit, argued that with the bunker reinforced by steel and timbers, scaling the rooftop now appeared to be too dangerous. Explosives, however, could do the job.

On May 7 an exasperated Mayor Goode made the first of what would be several key and fatal mistakes, when the police commissioner met with him to apprise him of the tactical plan. "You are the professional," Goode said. "You need not keep me informed of the details." Goode later would say that his main concerns were the protection of lives—civilian and police—and that officers who executed the plan not be "emotionally attached" to the events of 1978.

Meanwhile, community negotiators had been inside the house, where they spoke with Gerald Ford Africa, the "Minister of Information." On Friday, May 10, the negotiators told authorities there were hopeful signs: "Move wants out."

But the optimism faded fast on Saturday, when the cult insisted on an impossible demand: it would not leave the house unless all Move members convicted in the 1978 shootout were first released from prison. That day, a judge signed new search and arrest warrants charging Move members with illegal riot, firearms violations, and making terroristic threats. "Move is determined to provoke an armed confrontation and will resist with deadly force any effort to serve lawful process," a police affidavit filed with the warrants said.

At the police academy, bomb squad officers were now considering the use of explosives to blow out an opening somewhere in the Move house. The best option was to blast a hole in the common wall from the house next door and insert a gas-delivery machine directly into the Move house. There were two dangers in this: the possibility that Move had already broken through walls and had access to the houses on either side; that bullets could rip right through foot-thick walls.

The backup option had none of those problems. If the walls couldn't be breached to pump tear gas into the house, the roof could. A helicopter and explosives could do the job.

At City Hall the mayor's office distributed copies of a four-page hand-printed letter that Move member Ramona Africa had sent to the mayor. It sounded ominous:

"You can not surprise Move . . . any surprise attack on this house . . . will end up in not only you planners getting fucked up, but a whole lot of these neighbors getting fucked up." If police came in, she warned, it would be a "mess." And, "If Move go down, not only will everybody in this block go down . . . we will burn this house down and burn you up with us."

Warily, the mayor told the police department to proceed with its plan to force Move out.

Sunday, May 12, was Mother's Day. Neighbors on Osage Avenue strolled home from church; children played on the sidewalks in a warm sun. Even some of the Move kids were outside, raggedly dressed, squinting into the bright sky, staring at police helicopters that clattered noisily over rooftops.

Down the street, wooden barricades were being slapped into position. Knots of police officers gathered at various locations in the neighborhood. Throughout the day, police officers went door-to-door to homes in a six-block area surrounding the Move residence, telling people they had to be out of their houses by ten P.M. or face arrest. By midnight about three hundred people had been evacuated. Most carried belongings for what they had been told would be a one-night absence, and found lodging with relatives, friends, or in shelters set up by churches.

Inside the perimeter, a small team of community mediators had been shuttling back and forth all day between the Move house and police command headquarters, hoping to resolve the situation. But time was running out. One of the mediators, Novella Williams, spoke to the mayor on the phone Sunday night, pleading with him to call off the assault and allow negotiators to continue talking. "Your Honor, you can't allow this to happen. If you allow the attack to be made at 6221 Osage, they will not come out alive."

The mayor replied that he had "the best experts in the country on this, and that something had to be done about the situation. What good would giving you more time do? If I don't go in now, I will appear irresponsible."

She told him, "You can't kill those people. It would be wrong." She said the mayor hung up on her.

After one last fruitless visit to the Move house, she approached a group of reporters at the scene and told them wearily, "As far as the Move people are concerned, that's it. There is no compromise. Their position is, come in and get them."

All night long, as the police assault force grew grimly larger, the Move loudspeakers screeched: "Send in the FBI! Send in the CIA! Send in the FBI! We have something for you! Send in the SWAT team! Bring in machine guns! We're going to swat you the fuck down!"

The police department's four stakeout units— eighty officers in all—had been at their posts since midnight, augmenting a force of another two hundred uniformed cops and firefighters surrounding the house. Fire trucks and emergency vehicles lumbered into place at nearby intersections. Police bomb-squad officers crept into position in the common alley behind the Move house. As dawn's first light streaked the sky, sharpshooters could be seen poised tensely behind sandbags on the flat roofs of nearby row houses.

Another eviction notice was about to be served. Police who had been on hand for the last one in 1978 prayed that history wasn't about to repeat itself.

Shortly after dawn the Move loudspeaker blasted that it was time to get on with it.

"Cops, come on in and get this thing started. We're going to kill you motherfuckers. We're going to turn this city into a ghost town!"

Police Commissioner Gregory Sambor was on Osage Avenue to take command. Sambor, an official whose fondness for gold-braided caps and shiny brass uniform accessories once prompted a local newspaper to describe him as being "dressed as gaudily as a Third World admiral," took a bullhorn at 5:30 A.M. and made his announcement:

"Attention Move. This is America. You have to abide by the rules of the United States." He told the barricaded cultists—thirteen in all were now inside the house—that they had fifteen minutes to come out.

Move wasn't budging. "We ain't got a motherfucking thing to lose," the loudspeaker shot back. "Come and get us. Remember we killed Ramp. Is your insurance paid up? Your wives will cash them in after today, motherfuckers!"

Inside the house, one of the six children, a frail thirteen-year-old boy named Birdie Africa, was awakened by the commotion. He heard his mother, Rhonda Africa, shout: "If one house get it, all of these houses are going to get it!"

The males ordered the women and children into the bunker in the cellar. "It was like I was going to die," Birdie Africa would later recall. In fact, he would be one of only two people inside the house to survive.

Twin fire department water cannons were trained on the roof, blasting columns of water at the bunker. It didn't go down. A few minutes after six A.M. police started firing. Tear-gas canisters were lobbed into the backyard. A single-file squad of cops started down the alley.

From inside the house came a roar of automatic weapons fire. The battle was on.

* * *

Under fire, a team of officers forced their way into the next-door house at 6223 Osage. Move members could hear the shrill whine of drilling in the common wall. This was followed by an explosion. At 6223 Osage the cops scattered. The blast they had set to break through the wall did not do the job. From the other side, Move bullets tore through the wall back at them. A cop pointed an Uzi machine gun at the wall and blasted away.

In the Move house, water from firehoses was filling the bunker in the cellar, where the women and children huddled in soaked blankets. "Long live John Africa!" the children chirped on cue.

Mayor Goode was at home monitoring the attack with a small group of city officials and state legislators. As the mayor served orange juice, they watched the assault on television. It looked like a war zone on Osage Avenue, but there was no way of telling which way the battle was going.

On the second floor of 6223 Osage, bomb-squad cops struggled valiantly under gunfire, nauseous from the tear-gas fumes that were spreading from the canisters outside.

Finally, a charge broke an eighteen-inch hole through the wall. Two cops, Lieutenant Frank Powell and Officer William Klein, peered through the smoke and dust into a bedroom of the Move house, seeing no one. They pushed through a gas-delivery machine called a pepper fogger and switched it on. It didn't work. Then they tossed tear gas grenades into the Move house.

At the same time, other cops blasted into 6219 Osage, the house on the opposite side of the Move house. Inside, they encountered Move members crouching in the smoke and began taking heavy fire. A cop was hit and went down. His bulletproof jacket saved his life, but the word that a cop had been shot spread through the police command. Officers were exhausted, frightened, and now enraged.

At 7:20 A.M., Sambor ordered a cease fire. By then police had expended more than 10,000 rounds of ammunition.

The assault was being broadcast live on television. As the smoke drifted away during the lull, the Move house looked like it had been shelled by a battleship. The front porch was demolished. But the cult was still dug in.

On nearby rooftops, beyond the perimeter, neighbors could be seen watching the action, settling into a morning of war on lawn chairs set up on flat row-house roofs. Helicopters swooped overhead. On the street, cops slumped behind sandbags in sheer exhaustion. Rubble and grime was everywhere.

The police next tried to bring in a big construction crane to knock the house down. For over an hour workers struggled to maneuver the giant crane down the narrow street, but there wasn't enough room. Besides, no one wanted to drive it into a hail of bullets.

At the police academy bomb-squad headquarters, as frustration mounted on Osage Avenue, the backup plan—to somehow get tear gas onto the roof —was now the operative one. After all of the firing, after 650,000 gallons of water had been blasted at it, the bunker still stood on the Move house, a blatant reminder to the cops that they had so far accomplished almost nothing.

At two P.M., Commissioner Sambor and the mayor's top aide, Managing Director Brooks, conferred five blocks away at the command post near Cobbs Creek. As they met like two generals near a battlefield, a state police helicopter was busily landing and taking off from a grassy area off Cobbs Creek Parkway, providing surveillance reports on the house. The men discussed the possibility of going with the plan to use the helicopter to put a tear-gas charge onto the roof. They hurried back to the scene and studied the Move house through binoculars. The bunker loomed on the roof.

Goode had gone to City Hall, where he held a press conference at three P.M. and restated his determination. "We intend to evict them from the house. We will do it by any means necessary. I hope to God those children will not be injured. We will do everything that we can to prevent that."

Ninety minutes later on Osage Avenue, police escorted a middle-aged woman to a vantage point on 62nd Street, about a hundred yards from the house. She was Mary Clare Leak, the mother of Theresa Brooks Africa, one of the women inside the house. Nervously, the woman raised a bullhorn.

"Theresa, respond to me. This is the only chance I have to talk to you. Please come out with the children! You can't do this! Theresa, come out please before it's too late. The children are innocent victims, let them come out. They don't have a chance." The Move loudspeaker was mute.

* * *

The order was passed. At the police academy, where some of the bomb-squad officers who had been in combat on Osage Avenue now had reassembled, final preparations were under way on the hastily concocted plan to use a bomb to blow a hole in the roof, through which the gas would be inserted. A commercial explosive, Tovex TR2, was to be employed. Lieutenant Powell, who had been under heavy fire all morning, supervised the building of two bombs—one to be kept as a backup. Each consisted of Tovex, a gray jellylike substance, stuffed into a sixteen-inch tube, which was placed in a satchel with a tear-gas canister inside. The satchel was fitted with a 45-second fuse, a blasting cap, and an igniter.

Tovex TR2 was designed by its manufacturer, DuPont, for use in mining operations, where it was inserted into holes in the ground and ignited to excavate soil and underground rock. It was not meant for open-air use, DuPont would later say, in part because a Tovex explosion could generate heat approaching 7,000 degrees Fahrenheit.

At 5:10 P.M., Managing Director Brooks phoned the mayor and told him, "We have decided to blow the bunker off the roof, blow a hole in the roof, and put tear gas in."

Goode paused. "Does Mr. Sambor know about this?"

"Yes, it was his idea."

"Okay," said Goode. "Keep me posted." The mayor would later claim that he did not realize that with these words he had authorized the police to bomb a neighborhood.

* * *

Lieutenant Powell himself would drop the bomb. Just before 5:30, a blue and white Bell Jet Ranger helicopter, with a pilot, copilot, and Powell on board, came in over the low-slung rooftops and made four passes at the Move house in the middle of the block on Osage Avenue. On the fifth pass the helicopter hovered above the Move roof. Straining against his seat harness, Powell leaned out, pulled a cord, and dropped a green satchel onto the roof. It tumbled close to the bunker. As the chopper lifted away, it was buffeted by a great explosion that kicked smoke and debris thirty feet into the air.

From nearby rooftops and street corners hundreds of bystanders cheered lustily. But some shouted in horror. "They dropped a bomb on babies!" one man screamed. Like hundreds of thousands of others, the mayor watched on television.

The bunker was still standing. But the bomb had made a hole in the roof and smoke was pouring out. The smoke steadily thickened. Fifteen minutes later flames began licking at the roof. As firefighters waited, the flames spread. Move members began shooting again from the house.

At 6:19 P.M. police reported twenty-foot-high flames. Soon the flames were a hundred feet high. The front of the Move house began caving in. Around 6:30 fire hoses were trained on the flames. By seven P.M. the Move house and six adjoining houses were on fire, and the flames were spreading fast.

In the thick smoke billowing from the Move house, ghostly figures could be seen running for cover. The shooting kept up.

Behind the houses on Osage was an alley, sixteen

feet wide. Police sharpshooters, positioned at key points overlooking the alley, spotted two figures emerging from the back door of the Move house through a blanket of smoke. They were thirty-year-old Ramona Africa and the thirteen-year-old boy, Birdie, who was naked. As they stumbled outside, the boy tripped and fell into an eighteen-inch pool of water. Ramona tried to pull him out, but shots were being fired from the Move basement at cops who came into the open to offer help while their colleagues covered them with gunfire.

"I had enough! Don't shoot no more!" Ramona cried.

"Come to us. We're not coming to you," a cop bellowed from behind the wall across the alley.

Hollering at his colleagues to hold their fire, another officer dashed across, dodging Move bullets, and grabbed the badly burned child, pulling him to safety. The woman ran across the alley and was taken into custody.

The shadowy figures inside the house faded back into the billowing darkness. Police poured bullets into their receding forms.

At City Hall the mayor held forth on what everybody was watching on television. "What we have out there is war," he said. "I knew from the very beginning that once we made that decision to go in there, it would in fact be war." Goode said that the police commissioner had made the decision to drop what he called the "explosive device." The mayor said he himself was "fully accountable" for the decision.

By now, the entire 6200 block of Osage Avenue was engulfed in flames, and houses on adjoining streets were starting to burn. After six alarms had been called in, firefighters finally brought the fire under control at 11:41 P.M., six hours after it started.

In a late night press conference, a stunned Sambor said that police intelligence indicated that Move had built tunnels under the house, and this was the reason for the bomb being dropped. "In the morning we will go through the rubble and hope to find survivors," the police commissioner said.

There were none.

The neighborhood was in ruin, with more than sixty homes destroyed by fire as a result of the bomb dropped to blow a hole in the Move roof. With the exception of Ramona and Birdie Africa, everyone who had been in the Move house died, most of burns and suffocation, some of gunshot wounds.

Commissioner Sambor defended the bombing as a "tactical necessity" and said that Move had been threatening to create a terrorist incident that would "shock the nation, if not the world."

Likewise, the mayor told reporters, "You don't cry over spilt milk. We have to understand that sometimes we win and sometimes we lose." Mayor Goode said the authorities were afraid that Move would "blow up the entire neighborhood" and "create an international incident."

Ironically, it was Goode and his police force who created the international incident. The astonishing television pictures of an American neighborhood that had been bombed in order to save it were broadcast around the world. Never before in U.S. history had civil authorities dropped a bomb on an America city, and the reaction to the debacle was fierce. A columnist for the *Inquirer* asked sarcastically, "Who coordinated this thing—Moe, Larry, and Curley?"

"They broke every rule in the book," said Gerald Arenberg, the director of the American Federation of Police. "To burn down sixty homes in order to serve an eviction notice seems incredible."

"You don't just bomb a house!" gasped Hardy Williams, the Democratic state senator who represented the district. "It was stupid and tragic to bomb a house in the city. The Russians weren't coming!"

On Osage Avenue the grim work of digging through the rubble began. Now that the houses were destroyed, the giant crane could be maneuvered easily enough down the street, where it took up a position in front of what had been the Move house. For days the crane's monster scoop chewed into the stinking rubble, depositing the soggy debris onto a huge heap in the middle of the street. As the demolition went on, all that remained of the houses that had lined Osage Street were brick walls of varying heights towering over fields of blackened debris. The scene reminded some of the pictures of the German city of Dresden after the air-raid firestorms of the Second World War.

Rearing its head like a brontosaurus, the crane sometimes came up with body parts tangled in the debris, with blackened and twisted limbs, a child's torso, the charred carcasses of dogs.

Inside the house, in the mud of the twenty-foot-deep basement bunker, a worker dug a soggy tablet of paper out of the muck. On it was a note signed by none other than John Africa himself. Authorities had no idea how the founder of Move, long in hiding, had managed to slip back into the house for the final confrontation.

The crudely lettered note said that the police would come. "Pick them out one by one."

On Wednesday afternoon the crane's big scoop roared up with a grotesquely charred male corpse in its teeth. John Africa's body was dropped onto the junk heap, where workers from the medical examiner's office pulled it out and removed it for identification.

CHAPTER SIX

❧ ❧ ❧

Blood Atonement

JEFFREY DON LUNDGREN was thirty-four years old in 1984, a Navy veteran and religious fanatic who had chronic problems holding a steady job. Now he was ready for the big move.

He was mowing the grass outside the modest little house in Independence, Missouri, where he lived with his wife and four children, when it came to him.

Rushing inside the house, he found the citation he was looking for in a book of Mormon scripture in which the founder of Mormonism, Joseph Smith, reports that God told him:

". . . you should go to the Ohio, and there I will give unto you my law and there you shall be endowed with power from on high . . ."

Suddenly, all was clear. The repeated firings and dead-end jobs, the wife and in-laws who wondered if he was a born loser, the debts, the sullen-faced kids —God had *wanted* him to fail so that he could see the way. It was all part of the divine plan.

Jeff gathered around him his wife, Alice, and their

four children: Damon, fourteen; Jason, ten; Kristen, five, and Caleb, four. He said it was time to start packing. "We are going to Ohio," he exulted. "The Lord has chosen me for a great mission."

To finance the sudden move, he even sold off part of his prized gun collection.

Less than a month later, when the Lundgrens arrived in rural Kirtland, Ohio, with the threadbare family belongings piled into a U-Haul trailer, the puffy-faced man at the wheel of the old station wagon looked more like the stereotype of an American couch potato than he did a prophet. But make no mistake about it, a prophet is what he believed himself to be, and a very important one at that. He had come to Ohio to work diligently on a plan that he believed would bring about the end of the world.

Jeff would fail in that, as he had in everything else. But before he was apprehended in 1990, five people —a man, woman, and their three children—lay dead in a cold pit dug in the dirt inside a barn. Jeff and his cult of followers had put them there, preparing for Armageddon.

The Lundgrens' move from their home in Missouri had actually followed a series of religious visions experienced by Jeff, who had become impatient in recent years with what he regarded as liberalizing trends in the small sect of Mormonism to which he and his wife had belonged since birth. In the most dramatic of these visions, Jeff felt that he was bodily transported through time to Calvary, where Christ, dying on the cross, had fixed him with a long and baleful gaze.

"I looked at him and I knew, and he knew, that I had been rejecting him," Jeff had warned his wife before the move to Ohio. "I understand what it is like to be rejected, and he knew too."

"But what does it mean?" she asked.

"God is preparing me for something," he replied.

"What will you do?"

"Preside over the end of time," he said modestly.

Kirtland is an unlikely place from which to contemplate the destruction of the world. A bucolic farming community in the rolling landscape just beyond the urban sprawl of Cleveland, its main claim to fame is as the site of a historic Mormon temple that soars atop a hill on the northern edge of town. The Kirtland temple was built by the founder of Mormonism, Joseph Smith, and shortly after his death in 1844 it became the headquarters of a conservative sect of Mormons who had stayed behind in the Midwest while the mainstream Mormon following migrated to Utah. The Midwest branch called itself the Reorganized Church of Jesus Christ of Latter Day Saints—RLDS, in short.

Mormonism is a uniquely American religious movement that brims with the promise of earthly reward. It sprang from religious visions experienced in the 1820s by the teenage founder on his parents' farm in upstate New York. Joseph Smith told a strange tale that an angel named Moroni had appeared to him to disclose the hidden location of magical golden plates documenting the history of a band of ancient Hebrews who had migrated across the sea from Jerusalem to establish a civilization on the American continent, six hundred years before the birth of Christ. By the early 1830s, after he claimed to have unearthed and translated these golden plates into the Book of Mormon, Smith was declaring himself the Prophet, the designated one who would lead the lost tribe of Israel in the rebuilding of Zion and command the forces of righteousness in the final great battle against Satan that would herald the Second Coming, after which the faithful would join Jesus Christ to rule rapturously over an earthly paradise for a thousand years. The faithful were called the Latter Day Saints. Unbelievers, called Gentiles, were the doomed.

Joseph Smith had had several brushes with the law during his early ministry, having been implicated in counterfeiting and in the deception of a farmer in a buried treasure scheme. This did not adversely affect his later ability to recruit followers into a radical new religious sect. With its promise of a prosperous godly existence in this world, its emphasis on male domination and native-born white supremacy, its disdain for alcohol and smoking, and its preoccupation with Masonic-like secret rituals and symbols, Mormonism rapidly gained adherents in a conservative, restless agrarian society. The movement quickly migrated westward with the shifting farm population. Smith, always adept at raising cash, soon set up his headquarters—as commanded by God—in Ohio, in Kirtland, where he rewrote the entire Bible and, in 1836, on a fifteen-acre site atop a hill, built the first Mormon temple.

Smith kept moving westward, however, after God revealed to him that the actual site of the Second Coming would be Independence, Missouri. But the quest to establish a New Jerusalem met with fierce resistance in Missouri, where the Mormons' proclivities for real estate deals and banking speculation added to the simmering resentment over their practice of polygamy. Vilified, hounded by creditors, Smith himself was eventually murdered by an angry mob in 1844. The Prophet's death left the sect split between adherents of the founder—who vowed to continue pressing west, and ultimately settled in Salt Lake City, Utah, under the leadership of Smith's chief aide, Brigham Young—and those of Smith's eleven-year-old son, who remained behind at the temple in Kirtland.

Young's Utah Mormons became the mainstream Church of Jesus Christ of Latter Day Saints, eventually gathering more than five million members and vast financial holdings. The Ohio branch, renaming itself the Reorganized Church of Jesus Christ of Latter Day Saints, scratched out a meager existence around the site of Smith's temple in Kirtland, never numbering more than 200,000 members, most of them living in the Midwest, where they awaited the arrival of the next great prophet—whom they anticipated as the legitimate successor to Joseph Smith—to lead them to Judgment Day.

They were still waiting in 1984 when the Lundgrens lumbered into town.

On the day they arrived, Jeff and Alice went directly to the temple grounds in Kirtland and got jobs as members of the historic site's tour-guide staff—positions that qualified them to occupy a modest church-owned house near the temple grounds. However, Jeff was not a typical RLDS tour guide. Staring at the stately old temple in 1984, its stucco walls inlaid with crushed glass and porcelain that caused the building to glitter in the sunlight, he did not see just a venerable religious site that was the center of his religion. He saw divine opportunity.

Quietly, the Lundgrens settled in to their new life.

Millenialist religions, which believe that the end of the world is near and will herald a period of a thousand years of prosperity and justice for the chosen who have defeated Satan at Armageddon, have always attracted to their ranks people like Jeff Lundgren, who have a score to settle with the world.

The Book of Mormon, for example, says: "And it came to pass that the spirit said unto me, 'Slay him, for the Lord hath delivered him into thy hands. Behold the Lord slayeth the wicked to bring forth his righteous purposes . . .'"

Jeff was born in Independence in 1950 to well-off and stern RLDS sect parents who encouraged his intense youthful interest in interpreting Scripture. Some friends who grew up with him would describe him as a loner, a bitter young man who had few friends and an exalted opinion of his own status. Others, including a core of followers who would ultimately leave Independence to follow him to Kirtland, saw him as a visionary.

Not quite a year younger, Alice Lundgren had grown up in a trailer in Independence, where she was remembered as shy, homely, and even more desperate for status than her husband. Like him, she was deeply religious. In 1970, at church summer camp, she reported that she had been accosted in her bed by Satan. Shortly afterward, she met Jeff, and was immediately taken by his domineering presence, his fervent faith, his detailed knowledge of Scripture, and—most of all—his confidence.

Alice soon became pregnant; Jeff's parents denounced her, but not him. With the baby—a son, who would be named Damon—about to be born, Jeff enlisted in the Navy and was sent to San Diego. There, the young married couple found a cheap apartment outside the naval base, where they withdrew in horror from the freewheeling southern California lifestyle of the early seventies. Instead, the devout young couple spent their free time, when they weren't bickering over money or over Jeff's incessant demands for sex, reading the Book of Mormon aloud together. In time, their evangelism attracted a handful of kindred souls—typically conservative young couples who had grown up looking for religious comfort. The Lundgrens' tiny apartment became the location of weekly and then twice-weekly prayer-group meetings. Jeff led them avidly.

Briefly, in 1972, Jeff was stationed on board a Navy destroyer that spent about a month off Vietnam. The ship encountered a few rounds of hostile shore fire that splashed harmlessly into the sea. Although U.S. naval vessels never came under serious attack during the entire Vietnam War, in Jeff's mind the minor incident took on Battle of Midway-like dimensions.

"God showed me a sign," he would say of what he came to regard as a harrowing escape in combat conditions. "He had protected the ship because he didn't want me to die in Vietnam." Later, he would fantasize to his awestruck followers that he had been in furious hand-to-hand combat in Vietnam when God interceded to spare his life.

And not just from a mortal enemy. While at sea, Jeff experienced more vivid religious visions, not the least of which was one in which Satan attacked him from a cloud.

"I have always known from that moment that God had a special purpose for me," he told his wife shortly after they arrived in Kirtland. "But now I know that at last I am worthy."

As always, his wife assumed that he knew what he was talking about.

Jeff's supreme confidence had taken many years to attain. After his Navy discharge, he struggled to define his divine mission, while working odd jobs to support a growing family back in Independence, and often being fired. His fervid evangelism again attracted a small group of followers—young RLDS members, many of them, like the Lundgrens, disenchanted by church elders' attempts to broaden membership by liberalizing long-held positions toward women, traditionally relegated to a subservient role in Mormon church and family. When the RLDS actually proposed allowing women to become priests, Jeff and his followers in Independence coalesced into a small but radical dissident movement. If, as it appeared, the forces of Satan were assembling for the final battle, the army of the righteous needed a general, and Jeff Lundgren had come to regard himself as that person well before the decision to move to Ohio.

The preparations would take time. While contemplating Armageddon from its supposed site in Missouri, Jeff had managed to supplement his unsteady income by writing bad checks. A man of voracious appetites, he also began to have affairs.

Almost imperceptibly, the dozen or so adults who gathered at the Lundgrens had come to accept him as their leader. As his position solidified, Jeff manipulated group psychology to isolate and intimidate anyone who dissented. In the home, his authority was demonstrated in a less subtle way toward his wife and children—with the back of his hand.

In the bedroom, meanwhile, Jeff was less prophet than pervert, his wife would later claim. While he complained constantly of her frigidity, she found it difficult to enjoy sex with a chronically unfaithful husband who also, she said, collected sadomasochistic pornography and liked to tie her up and defecate on her breasts.

"Jeffrey was fascinated with his own feces," she would tell investigators. "He would smear it on himself and masturbate with it." On one occasion, she said, he dressed up in her nightgown, panty hose, and hair rollers and demanded that she act out raping him with a dildo. Alice also later claimed that Jeff beat her repeatedly.

Projecting an air of religious mysticism, Jeff managed to keep both family and followers firmly in place.

In Ohio, galvanized by his sense of mission, he surreptitiously began recruiting, and organizing an army of God. It would require stealth, money, and years of planning to outwit the forces of Babylon under their very eyes in the temple. But Jeff was well-positioned to do it. As temple tour guides, lecturing to the hundreds of RLDS pilgrims who visited the historic site each day, he and Alice quietly recruited, and Jeff stealthily took advantage of easy access to the donation boxes as well as the cash drawers at the gift shop and bookstore. Before the Lundgrens were ousted three years later, when temple elders discovered the missing funds, Jeff would manage to walk off with about $20,000 in petty cash to help finance his plan to reclaim the temple from Satan.

Meanwhile, he had diligently used his popular tours, augmented by his role leading a well-attended Bible class, to firmly establish a secret group of several dozen RLDS dissidents before the church's elders realized what was going on.

Situated close to the pilgrimage site, the Lundgren household was always open to those who believed. Accepting room and board, or merely seeking company and spiritual uplift, men and women gathered nightly for Jeff's religious instructions. During the day, the adults worked in whatever local jobs they could find, including as part-time temple tour guides. Some referred to Jeff, the head of the household, as "Dad," and to his wife as "Mother."

While luxuriating in unaccustomed if moderate financial stability, Jeff managed to find plenty of time at the temple to diagram scriptural verses and wander the building indulging his fascination for deciphering secret meanings in the intricately carved ritualistic symbols that decorated the somber rectangular chambers. In the blazing intensity of an obsessed mind, the patterns became inexorably more striking.

In the autumn of 1986 he excitedly told Alice that he now knew that he was the last of eight great prophets who had lived since the beginning of time. In a vision, Joseph Smith himself appeared to him to declare that the torch was being passed, that he, Jeff Lundgren, the greatest prophet of all, had been chosen at the beginning of time to bring about the kingdom of God on earth.

Alice was thrilled. "Jeffrey had finally found a niche in life," she would later say. "I decided he was truly my lord and master."

Given to gossip herself, she had difficulty keeping this revelation from the regulars in Jeff's prayer groups, as he said she must for the time being.

"I have a secret," she once giddily told the faithful group after Jeff had finished a four-hour harangue and wandered off to the bedroom in exhaustion. "But I can't tell you yet what is in store for us all."

Since it was well-understood that discussion of Jeff's teaching outside his supervision was absolutely forbidden, no one asked for details. Jeff insisted that, like Christ, he would merely intimate his divinity. It would be for the disciples to arrive at the truth on their own.

Jeff's growing folk-hero reputation among restive RLDS followers in Kirtland finally did get the attention of RLDS elders, who were anxious about rumors of heresy being spread in the Lundgren prayer group. But the president of the RLDS in Kirtland, Reverend Dale Luffman, a soft-spoken and modest man not given to direct challenges, urged caution as the Lundgren contingent drifted into what would soon become an open break. Luffman had no idea of how divisive that break was about to become.

* * *

The rift opened with the discovery of the missing money. A visiting church official, curious about the drop-off in cash receipts, looked over the gift shop and visitor center books in the summer of 1987 and discovered the odd coincidence that the three-year decline in revenue—a total of about $20,000—had begun shortly after Jeff and Alice came to work at the temple. But with no evidence linking Jeff directly to the thefts, and hoping to avoid a public scandal, RLDS officials visited the Lundgrens and offered Jeff a quiet way out. If he and Alice would resign, there would be no accusations. They would have to vacate their church-owned house, but they could leave without recrimination.

Jeff presented himself as a scapegoat, falsely accused and persecuted by treacherous RLDS elders who wanted to destroy his efforts to preach the truth. The embezzlement episode merely enabled him to tighten his hold on the dissident group and isolate people under his control even further. The Lundgrens rented a ramshackle five-bedroom farmhouse isolated on fifteen acres of land at the southern edge of town. Beside the house, along a muddy apple orchard, stood a dilapidated red barn. There was plenty of ground for training. It was the perfect place for a commune. Jeff and Alice spoke of plans to make the homestead self-sustaining; they would prosper, growing their own food, perhaps even starting an antiques business in the barn.

Furthermore, banishment from the temple was merely another prophesy fulfilled. "The Scriptures say that prophets are cast out," Jeff informed the group. "That is happening."

An impressive arsenal of guns had been accumulated by this time. Throughout 1986 and 1987 the group had been buying weapons, using them in paramilitary training for the assault on the temple.

Meanwhile, Jeff had pored over the temple's cryptic symbols and endlessly diagramed verses of Scripture, looking for the hidden clues. Late in the summer of 1987, he had made the long-awaited announcement. "I am the last messenger that God has sent to the Kirtland temple to prepare the way for Christ's return," he said. "And you are going to help me protect it."

After the move to the farm, where he was free from the proprieties necessitated by living on church property, Jeff's message became even more strident, alarmist, and violent. Cannily, he instilled a sense of impending crisis and drama over the armed assault on the temple, which would be heralded by an explosion of nature: earthquakes would rend the ground; the temple would be physically lifted high onto a mountain. Then the legions of Satan would storm Kirtland, perhaps led by battalions of U.S. Army troops seeking to unite with the evil forces within the temple. As prophet, Jeff told his followers that if they were "free of sin," God would give them the means to repel these armies.

The paramilitary training in the apple orchard drew some outside attention, but no one really understood the level of insanity that the Lundgren group was spiraling toward in its farmstead isolation. However, getting wind of the rumors that Lundgren's heretical teachings had taken on violent overtones, Reverend Luffman finally took the drastic step of excommunicating Jeff, Alice, and their two older sons, Damon and Jason, from the RLDS.

A few days after this action, the area was hit with a violent thunderstorm, after which a double rainbow appeared in the sky. Jeff pounced on the weather as a grave new sign—the fabled seven seals described in the Book of Revelation were being broken open, one by one.

There was time to prepare, however. In the near future, he suddenly announced, they all would have to leave Kirtland for a period of time, "living off the land" in the wilderness. Jeff said that they would have one year to "show blood" and break the remaining seals to open the way to Armageddon.

"There will be lots of blood spilled," he confided.

The Luffman family's blood would be first, according to Jeff's plan. When the time came to take the temple, he declared, Luffman would be the first one captured. He would be bound and gagged, then forced to watch the execution of his wife Judy and their three children, ages thirteen, ten, and five. Then he would be killed.

In general, the Lundgren group kept to itself, out of sight on the farm. But Luffman wasn't the only one with serious concerns. Rumors of armed men playing soldier are sure to interest the local police, and the chief of the six-member Kirtland police force, Dennis Yarborough, himself an RLDS member, had decided to play closer attention to whatever was going on at the Lundgren place. Yarborough had thought there was something odd about Jeff Lundgren from the first day he laid eyes on him, back in 1984, when Jeff—newly arrived at the temple—

barged into the police station shouting that people were peeking into his windows at night. Jeff later painted the windowpanes of the house dark green.

Now, aware of the rumors about Jeff's resignation from his temple job, and deeply curious about reports of weapons stockpiling and the wild rumors about storming the temple, Yarborough visited Lundgren to look things over and ask about the "paramilitary group" that had been seen training in the apple orchard. Jeff said he knew nothing about it.

From that point on, the police chief and the Lundgren group kept their eyes on each other from a distance.

What little of a disturbing nature that people had seen on the outside was no indication of the true emotional deterioration within a frightened, exhausted, and fanatically loyal group who saw enemies everywhere outside their own numbers. Besides Jeff, Alice, and their children, five unmarried adults now lived in the farmhouse, with their numbers supplemented by married couples with children who lived in nearby apartments.

Residing at the farmhouse were:

• Kevin Currie, who had arrived in Kirtland on a pilgrimage in 1984 and moved in with the Lundgrens, whom he had known from their study group in San Diego.

• Richard Brand, a well-muscled man in his mid-twenties, an unemployed civil engineer who fell in with the Lundgrens during a pilgrimage to the temple in 1985. Richard had a new pickup truck that he was willing to sell for $5,500, and donate the money to the Lundgrens.

• Shar Olsen, tall and pretty, in her late twenties, met the Lundgrens when she toured the temple in 1987. Though Jeff was particularly attracted to her, Shar was the most skeptical of the group—and would prove to be the most troublesome.

• Danny Kraft, born in Iowa in 1964, he was an aspiring musician with a lifelong fascination with symbols and Mormon archaeology. He joined the group after taking one of Jeff's temple tours in 1985.

• Sharon Bluntschly, born in 1958. At 225 pounds, she was withdrawn and painfully shy. She met the Lundgrens on a temple pilgrimage in 1985.

And these followers lived in apartments:

• Greg Winship, a childhood friend of Richard Brand, a business major in college who was introduced to Jeff Lundgren as a "prophet" when he visited Richard in 1986.

• The Patrick family: Dennis and Tonya Patrick, fellow church members who had moved to Kirtland in 1986 at the invitation of Jeff and Alice. Both in their early thirties, they had been members of Jeff's prayer group in Independence. Dennis was tall, skinny, and meek. Tonya was heavyset, pretty, and vivacious. Jeff disliked Dennis but was attracted to his wife. The Patricks had a six-year-old daughter, Molly.

• The Luff family: In their late twenties, Ron and Susie Luff and their two children, Matthew, five, and Amy, two, had joined the Lundgrens from Independence in 1987. He was nervous and wiry; she was slender, attractive, and chatty.

• The Avery family: Dennis and Cheryl Avery and their three young daughters had moved to Kirtland from Independence to join the Lundgrens shortly before the move to the farm. Cheryl was plain and brooding, but with a sharp tongue. Dennis was fussy, pudgy, and pedantically argumentative, but essentially submissive, especially in the company of other men.

In all cultlike groups, certain people or persons inevitably become scapegoats on whom other members of the organization can focus their rage, disappointment, and frustration when things inevitably go wrong. Haplessly, the Averys would play such a role in the Lundgren cult.

Dennis and Cheryl Avery referred to the Lundgrens as their best friends, unaware that Jeff and Alice ridiculed them mercilessly behind their backs. Jeff especially disliked Dennis, whom he thought dim-witted and dominated by his wife.

Alice had in fact tried to dissuade Jeff from encouraging the Averys to move to Kirtland, but Jeff had his reasons.

"I want their money," he told her, aware that the Averys would realize about $20,000 profit from the sale of their house in Independence.

It paid off. Not long after they arrived, Dennis gave Jeff a check for $10,000. But Jeff was furious that the Averys had apparently used the rest of their profit to pay off bills and buy things to furnish the apartment they rented in Kirtland.

* * *

The facade of an idyllic communal life barely covered a reality of daily drudgery. The farm was badly run-down. Members worked hard fixing it up and performing chores on their free time. As the prophet's wife, Alice, was accorded deferential treatment and expected to be catered to and waited on by the other women. She lay around the house most days drinking beer, watching television, gobbling take-out food, barking orders, and screaming at the other couples' children. Her major group responsibility was the only chore she willingly performed: she shopped.

In fact, both of the Lundgrens were dedicated shoppers. Jeff's favorite haunts were gun shops, video stores, and home centers; Alice's were discount stores and antiques shops.

Jeff had designated his eldest son, Damon, as his second-in-command. A sullen, lazy youth who was a member of the high school wrestling team, Damon was in charge of physical training within the group. The young man, who had learned bullying techniques from his father, was especially fond of ordering one male member to fall to the ground in training and kiss his feet.

This kind of activity only reinforced the submissiveness that Jeff had already ruthlessly imprinted on the psyches of the other male believers.

Even the younger Lundgren children claimed special status. They were referred to as the "naturals," and could not be corrected by anyone. Children of all other members were the "unnaturals."

The lengthy nightly religious study sessions—now conducted in the drafty barn—deteriorated into angry denunciations and recriminations directed toward anyone whose attention wandered, or who failed to come up with correct answers to Jeff's incessant metaphysical questions.

Along with the harangues, Jeff required the group to watch rented VCR movies nearly every night. Most nights, the movies were war epics and bloody, Rambo-type thrillers, but Jeff occasionally changed the pace and rented old Hollywood romantic films—to show, he said, how women could better become "submissive."

But romance had little priority by 1989. Again and again Jeff said, "God is commanding us to take over the Kirtland temple." The battle would be long and arduous, he warned. "We will have to live off the land" while protecting the temple, he said. He began referring to himself as the "destroyer." Scripture itself proved that "God is not afraid to kill," he maintained.

Military training moved out of the orchard. On some moonless nights the men—clad in dark fatigues, their faces blackened with paint—engaged in guerrilla-type covert exercises on the grounds of the temple itself. Military code names were assigned to each of them. During the assault on the temple, not only the Luffman family would die. Every person living in a one-block area near the temple—in all, more than two dozen members of RLDS families—would be beheaded.

By 1989 the sessions were often lasting all night. Jeff, now constantly with a pistol on his belt or waving in his hand, had designated himself a four-star general in command of what he called the "Army of Israel." As befit his status, Alice—who also had begun drinking, something virtually unheard-of for a devout Mormon—roused herself enough to sew him a flag—a white star and an eagle on a background of regal purple.

The other women learned how to clean and care for weapons. Supervision at the farm became vigilant. When Jeff was away from the house, a "sheriff" was designated to oversee the group. Mail and telephone calls were strictly monitored. Everyone outside was the enemy, the "Gentiles."

As these bizarre preparations intensified, the Averys made a fatal mistake that would significantly alter the Lundgren battle plan: they began complaining about money.

With mounting financial problems, the Averys strongly implied that since they had donated so much money to Jeff, he owed them additional financial consideration. After Jeff publicly denounced them for their presumption, the Averys began missing some of the nightly meetings. Without knowing it, they were scapegoated in their absence.

Only those without sin could take part in the temple assault, Jeff stressed—and the Averys were not without sin. But it wasn't just the Averys, he said. Other members would be found not worthy before the final plan went into effect. Only he could read their souls, Jeff said, and know who they might be.

To atone in blood for their sins, they would be killed.

At one point Jeff claimed that only twelve adults— the same number as the apostles—would survive along with him. While he refused to name them in group sessions, in several private conversations he assured people of their own safety. Later, when survivors compared notes, they would learn that the names of those who would be spared kept changing, depending on whom he was talking to.

But the unwelcome Averys and their "disrespectful" children were certainly at the top of the list of the condemned.

"By not attending my classes, the Averys have hardened their hearts to the word," Jeff said, making every effort to ostracize the Averys as traitors, even though the Averys were making every effort to return to the group's good graces.

Years later, from death row in prison, Jeff would tell Pete Earley, author of *Prophet of Death: The Mormon Blood Atonement Killings:* "I told my people they should thank God for the Averys . . . God had provided the Averys to us to be used as sacrifices."

The others marveled at the Averys' obliviousness to the peril they were in. While behind their backs Jeff was discussing killing them, the Averys were whining about being owed money and not being invited to dinner.

There were two key defections from the group at about this time. The first was Kevin Currie, who fled when he decided he was among those designated to die.

The next was Shar Olsen, who had become alarmed by the buildup of weapons in the house, and troubled by doubt about Jeff's claims to being the last prophet.

Both Kevin and Shar left and independently approached authorities to report their fears about Jeff Lundgren's plan to storm the temple. Quietly, police surveillance of the Lundgren farm was stepped up.

Jeff recruited several new members to make up for the defections. One was Debbie Olivarez, a cousin of Jeff's who worked as a nurse at a local hospital.

Additionally, a new family moved to Kirtland and joined the group in March 1989: Larry Keith and Kathy Johnson and their four children. The Johnsons also had been associated with the Lundgren prayer group in Independence.

But the plans were changing, thanks in part to the opportunity for retribution presented by the Averys. While the police worried about rumors of an armed assault on the Kirtland temple, the Lundgren group prepared to flee to the wilderness.

Since blood had to be shed to fulfill prophecy and cleanse the group, the killing plan was refined under Jeff's increasingly erratic direction. Men designated to die would be beheaded, but those with wives and children would watch them die first, he said. Adult females were to be stripped naked and disemboweled with a sword. Children were to be picked up by their heels and have their skulls smashed against a wall.

Soon the plan was simplified to focus just on the Averys. They would be killed and all of the others would flee to the wilderness, where they would wait for the sign to assault the temple.

This required frantic shopping for outdoor clothing, camping gear, guns, and used vehicles to carry the hardy band into the wilderness, although none of them had any idea where they would be going. But evidentally it would not be far, since Jeff and Alice—who alone would decide—were seen studying maps of Ohio and West Virginia.

There were many so small details. For instance, Becky Avery, who had just turned thirteen years old, presented Jeff with a dilemma. He wondered aloud whether she should be considered a child or an adult for the purposes of the killing.

Alice suggested that "it would depend on whether or not Becky had started her period." Jeff mused that this was something that would need to be found out, and went back to his maps.

By the spring of 1989 there were more than two dozen members of the Lundgren cult who expected to go to the wilderness.

In early April, Jeff made a great show of going at dawn to a hilltop on the farm where he often retreated for personal guidance from God.

"What is thy will?" he cried out to the slate-gray sky. "Give me a sign!"

On April 10, Jeff ordered Keith and Ron to start digging a grave in the dirt floor of the barn. It was for the Averys.

A few nights later, seemingly full of forgiveness, Jeff and Alice had dinner at the Averys to discuss the trip to the wilderness. The next day, Jeff told officials at the Kirtland elementary school that the Avery children would miss school for a week. He said he was taking the family to Disney World.

The pit was to be finished on April 16, the day designated for the execution. But on the fifteenth, Dennis Avery, overjoyed at the opportunity to regain Jeff's good graces, came to the farm and happily showed Jeff a MasterCard he had just managed to acquire. It had a $1,000 limit.

After dinner Jeff told his wife that the Averys had

bought themselves some extra time on earth. "I'm going to take that boy shopping," he said.

He did. He and Dennis ran up the $1,000 limit on the new credit card, buying several guns—including an electric stun gun. After the shopping trip, Dennis felt that all was forgiven when Jeff told him to bring his family to the farm the next day—Monday, April 17. Within days, he said, they all would leave for the wilderness.

At the farm that night, Jeff took Richard aside. "Tomorrow is D-Day," he said.

On Monday the excitement level was high at the farm as the final preparations for the trip were made. The children were giddy at the prospect of what they considered would be an extended vacation.

The Averys arrived for dinner like relatives visiting at Thanksgiving. Little Karen Avery had even drawn a picture in crayon for Alice. Giggling, the child pressed it into her hand at the front door.

At a congenial dinner with everyone crowded around the huge table, the same child happened to get Jeff's attention when she refused to eat her corn. "Daddy, I don't want to," she protested.

Jeff watched with cold satisfaction. It was a sign of "rebellion and wickedness," he would later say. It was just further proof of what had to be done.

After dinner, as the other women went to the kitchen to clean up, Alice announced that she had to leave for the store to buy some last minute supplies. She took her own children—Jason, Kristen, and Caleb—out with her. Damon stayed behind.

"Call before you come back," Jeff said as his wife and younger children filed out.

Jeff left the table and went to his bedroom. Several of the other men came in and found him with a pistol in his hand, a .45 caliber. Dennis Avery was still eating with the women and children.

"Let's do it," Jeff said.

Dennis, busy with a second helping of dinner, did not comment as the rest of the men—Jeff, Damon, Richard, Ron, Danny, and Greg—went out to the old barn. There, they stood beside the pit that had been dug, four feet deep, six feet wide, eight feet long. It was big enough.

When Jeff gave a nod, Ron went inside to fetch Dennis from the table. He said Jeff wanted to see him in the barn.

When Dennis entered, one of the men grabbed him. Ron pressed the electric stun gun against his neck and pulled the trigger.

"This isn't necessary!" Dennis shouted as he fell backward. He was grabbed by four others, who had been hiding in the dark. They bound him with duct tape on his hands, feet, and mouth. A single lightbulb dangling from a wire in the ceiling was snapped on. Dennis saw himself being held at the edge of a pit.

Jeff approached him, looking steadily into his eyes, and leveled the .45 at his heart. Avery fell to his knees. Jeff squeezed the trigger two times.

The door opened.

"Is it done?" a man asked.

"Come and see what death is!" Jeff called.

The men stood silently.

"Okay," he said, "bring out the next one."

Ron went to the farmhouse and told Cheryl Avery,

helping to clean up, that her husband needed to see her in the barn.

She was set upon as Dennis had been, her hands, feet, and mouth taped, as well as her eyes—Jeff had said that Scripture dictated that only the man had the right to see his executioner.

"Be calm," she was told in her last seconds. "Don't struggle. Just give it up."

They threw her into the pit on top of her husband's blood-soaked body. Jeff shot her three times, twice in the chest and once in the belly. She lay writhing for several minutes.

Jeff went outside to get a breath of fresh air with the others. He was worried that neighbors might have heard the shots, but no one was stirring across the fields.

"Bring out the next one," he said.

Trina Avery, fifteen years old, was reading a magazine in the living room when Ron came for her.

"Your mother wants to see you out in the barn," he said.

Trina was subdued, as her mother had been. But the men told her it was a game as they taped her hands, feet, and eyes. She submitted without protest.

Two of the men carried her through the barn to the edge of the pit. She was laid down in the grave. Jeff stepped forward and shot her once in the head, and then twice more in the back as she struggled to climb out.

When she was still, they went back to the house and found the other two children, Becky and Karen, playing a video game in the living room.

"Who wants to see the horses in the barn?" Ron boomed merrily.

Both of them did.

"One at a time," he insisted.

Being thirteen, Becky went first. In the barn, she was bound and dragged to the pit, where Jeff shot her. The child died groping for her mother's body beneath that of her older sister's.

The six-year-old came next. Karen was made to sit blindfolded at the muddy edge of the pit. Then Jeff fired a hollow-point slug into her skull. He fired again, trying to hit the same place. The little girl toppled into the pile of bodies now filling the bloody grave.

The men slit open a bag of lime and emptied it over the corpses. Gingerly, they shoveled dirt on top, and then piled on rocks and debris that had been gathered in the barn for the purpose of hiding the grave.

As they tidied up, Jeff was out in the apple orchard gazing to the twilight sky.

"God, I have been thy sword of judgment this day," he bellowed at the gloom. "May my offering be acceptable!"

He then came back to the barn and assured the men, "Now that the sin is gone, we can go into the wilderness and see God."

They did not see God, nor did they even see the wilderness. Instead, the group frantically packed its belongings and drove off in several vehicles, finally assembling a few days later at a run-down public campsite in the Appalachian plateau of West Virginia. They pitched their tents in muddy ground that had been landfilled by a strip-mine operation.

Shortly after they fled, the police arrived for an

unannounced visit to the farm, hoping to check for weapons violations. They found no one there. They did not find the grave.

Through a cold spring and summer, the Lundgren group lived in campgrounds, where Jeff proclaimed himself Moses and made incessant sexual demands on the women. Gradually, misery and wretchedness triumphed over faith and fear, and people began leaving. Meanwhile, police investigating the group's disappearance found the bodies.

By the time Moses came back from his wanderings in the wilderness, only his wife and a few adult stragglers remained with him. And all were under arrest.

A county grand jury indicted Jeffrey, Ron, Richard, Damon, and Danny for aggravated murder, a crime punishable in Ohio by death. Dennis Patrick, along with Alice, Greg, Susie, Tonya, Sharon, and Kathy, were charged with conspiracy to commit murder.

Later, the prosecutor's office offered a deal to allow Richard to plead guilty to simple murder and Greg to complicity, in exchange for their testimony.

At one of the trials, the defense attorney argued that Jeff was a victim himself, an "emotionally abused" child who had suffered all his life from low self-esteem and had fixed on the Averys because Dennis Avery reminded him of his own shameful inadequacies. But Jeff sounded a more assured note in his own five-hour courtroom harangue, proclaiming himself a "prophet of God" and warning of retribution on sinners. It took the jury less than two hours to find him guilty of five counts of aggravated murder. The judge sentenced him to die in the electric chair. He is still awaiting execution.

Damon was found guilty of aggravated murder. The others all pleaded to avoid trial, except for Ron Luff, who was found guilty of murder and kidnapping and sentenced to 170 years in prison. Tonya, Dennis, and Kathy were permitted to plead to obstruction of justice, and given minimal sentences.

Alice, despite a defense partly predicated on allegedly being a battered woman, was convicted of conspiracy to commit aggravated murder. At her trial she insisted she did not know what Jeff was planning. "Everyone knew but me!" she wailed. But in a videotaped statement she had made when she was arrested, the jury had heard her say, "You had to be stupid not to know what he was up to."

No one believed Alice was stupid, least of all the judge, who sentenced her to 150 years in prison. Led out of the courtroom, she cried to the crowd, "I am not the Angel of Death!"

Later, in prison, Alice would recall without emotion the childish drawing that six-year-old Karen had given her when the Averys came to dinner on the night they all were killed. It was a picture of a rainbow, its rays brightly colored with crayons. On the bottom the little girl had scrawled, "To Alice—I love you. Karen."

CHAPTER SEVEN

❧ ❧ ❧

El Padrino

MARK KILROY WAS any parent's pride, a good-looking twenty-one-year-old with manners and brains, well-liked, a premed student with a ready smile that said he knew he was going somewhere in life. That promising life ended in the most grisly way possible, when he stopped at the Mexican border one night, apparently just to be polite to a stranger.

The end of Mark's short and happy life was grim proof that horror doesn't always have a prelude. One minute he was in the company of close friends he had known since grade school. The next, he was in the hands of the devil.

The nightmare had begun innocently enough, during spring break 1989, along the sunny beaches of the Gulf of Mexico. Like a quarter million other college-age kids, Mark and some friends had headed down to South Padre Island, a resort town on the Gulf just outside of Brownsville, at the heel of Texas. The trip to the spring bacchanal at South Padre was a major excursion for the boys, who had to drive all night down the Texas coast to get there. Mark's close high school buddy Brent Martin was at the wheel of his Olds Cutlass. In the back seat were Bradley Moore and Bill Huddleston. All of the boys had been working hard at college and looking forward to a rollicking vacation.

They checked into the Sheraton, but had no intention of spending much time in the room. Like their fellow revelers, the boys spent the days sunbathing on a beach overrun with college boys and girls, and their nights cruising the strip and partying. On a couple of nights, like thousands of others, they ventured in small groups across the Rio Grande to enjoy the less expensive and more freewheeling atmosphere of Matamoros, the dusty Mexican city that huddles close to the U.S. boundary and entices spring breakers with boisterous bars, thumping live music, cheap beer, and no minimum drinking age. For those so inclined, there are more lurid attractions available in Matamoros—prostitutes, drugs, sex shows. In Matamoros, it was said, anything goes.

Because of international car insurance restrictions, most Americans park on the Texas side of the border, walk through the customs portals, and hop into one of the dozens of tiny Mexican cabs always waiting on the other side for the short drive into the clutter and clamor of Matamoros. This is what the four youths did on Monday night, March 13, leaving the Cutlass in the vast parking lot on the U.S. side and piling into a cab for the ride into Matamoros. Mark and his pals were clean-cut kids, adventuresome enough to enjoy the border-town attractions, but not foolhardy enough to ignore the often repeated warnings: Violence from the border towns was already spilling over into places like Brownsville, and everyone knew not to venture alone into Matamoros at night.

Mark, especially, was no fool. "I know just enough Spanish to get into trouble, but not enough to get out," he had recently joked in the self-deprecating way that people admired about him.

There is no reason whatever to believe that on this night the boys did anything other than bar-hop, drink, laugh, swagger, and listen to music.

Late in the evening, as throngs of weary revelers head back home into the U.S., the Mexican streets leading to the border-crossing plaza between Matamoros and Brownsville are crowded bumper-to-bumper with taxicabs, motorcycles, cars, pickups, and bicycles. The sidewalks are jammed with clamoring peddlers hawking a bewildering array of wares—jewelry, ceramics, piñatas, burritos, fireworks, blankets, straw hats, cold beer, papier-mâché tropical birds on a stick. Especially during spring break, when Matamoros competes feverishly with more staid Brownsville and South Padre for the college students' dollars, the plaza is also filled with street hustlers—prostitutes trying to entice customers for one final fling in the shadows, drug dealers offering that last minute impulse purchase for anyone brazen enough to try to get it past U.S. customs, con men looking for one more score before the customers disappear over the border.

Mark and his friends were among the mob of returning revelers on that night, filing into place in the long lines of Americans snaking toward the customs gates at the middle of the plaza as the peddlers and hustlers worked the thick crowd like street vendors outside a rock concert.

Exhausted from a night of partying and beer, not particularly alert, looking forward only to bed, the boys drifted separately into several of the long lines waiting to pass through customs. There was a social protocol to the scene: Hustlers routinely approached you, and you politely (but firmly) said no thanks. Under the protocol, there was no badgering—the hustler merely moved on and approached someone else in line. It was business.

The wait to get through customs was about fifteen minutes that night. On the U.S. side the boys reassembled on the floodlit sidewalk to walk to the parking lot. But they couldn't see Mark anywhere in the sea of faces around them.

"Where's Mark?" someone said.

"He was right beside me before we went through customs," Bill said. "Maybe he went back to the car already."

Though he didn't think much about it at the time, Bill recalled a fleeting image he'd had of Mark—in fact, it would be the last one he would know of his friend. As they were shuffling ahead in the lines on the Matamoros side of the plaza, Bill noticed a young Mexican man step out from a knot of people on the street and approach Mark, who was in a slower line several rows away.

Bill hadn't paid much attention, since being approached was so routine. He'd heard the stranger say something like, "Hey man, you want . . . ?" He thought he saw Mark turn and step a few feet out of line to reply to the stranger, or perhaps to hear him better above the noise. Then the crowd edged forward, listlessly filling in the blank spaces in Bill's sight line. As they filed through customs, Bill assumed Mark was still among them.

But Mark wasn't waiting at the car. The boys looked for him in the parking lot, but there was no sign. It simply was not like Mark to wander off without a word. Worried now, they crossed back through customs, searched the Mexican side of the plaza, and then took a taxicab back into Matamoros. All night long they combed the now-deserted bars and walked the seedy main drag and dirty side streets, inquiring about an American boy. No one knew a thing.

As dawn approached, the only explanation that made sense was that perhaps Mark had been delayed at customs and then found his own ride back to the hotel. But the customs officers knew nothing about him, and when the boys drove to the hotel, he wasn't there. Could he have met a girl and be spending the night somewhere else?

The boys slept fitfully for only a few hours. Mark's absence simply didn't figure, not for a guy as conscientious as he. Mark would have called or left a message.

In fact, he would leave their lives without any further word. As they searched for their friend, finally calling Mark's parents, who notified police on both sides of the border, they had no way of suspecting the terrible truth. Mark Kilroy, who had only wanted to be polite, had been abruptly kidnapped from a public place. Before anyone knew what had happened, he was pushed into a car, tied up, and driven to a foul-smelling shack on a forlorn ranch south of Matamoros. His captors were a drug-dealing cult, one of the most feared gangs in northern Mexico.

They had snatched Mark off the street simply because they needed a young American male to mutilate and offer up as a human sacrifice in a black-magic ritual.

Within days Mark's parents, James and Helen Kilroy, along with a small group of relatives and friends, were familiar figures desperately canvassing the Matamoros area. As they searched, they began hearing disturbing reports that other young men had been reported missing—Mexican men, even young boys. Beyond the brazen commerce of the border town, Matamoros and its environs were a landscape of brutal poverty, besieged in recent years by warring drug gangs, where violence had grown as common as smoke from a chimney. Still, young men who otherwise stayed out of trouble had never before disappeared without a trace—even the ruthless local drug gangs tended to leave evidence of their violent work.

A concerned U.S. customs officer named Oran Neck worked on his off hours helping the small group of people looking for Mark. They combed the streets and back alleys of Matamoros, handing out flyers that had the young man's picture on them and offered a reward of $5,000. American helicopters buzzed the border scrublands, clattering low over the shallow Rio Grande, looking for a body.

As the search dragged on, they heard reports of other people who had simply disappeared from the area, people without well-financed families to alert the authorities. In Matamoros Mark's parents met a local couple, Isidoro and Ericada Garcia, who told them their fourteen-year-old son, José Luis Garcia Luna, had been missing since the same time Mark disappeared. Worse, other people whispered rumors about a mysterious new drug gang that had been taking over business in the region. The gang had supernatural powers, people whispered: its members could not be killed with human bullets. And it also had temporal protection, they confided, since membership included *federales*, members of the Mexican federal police.

The rumors were confounding and frustrating to a group of rational people trying to find a missing young man in a place where corruption breeds cynicism, where superstition, magic, and incantations are called on to explain things that reason cannot.

Meanwhile, as the searchers for Mark Kilroy stumbled around this wilderness of cracked mirrors, in a town not far away two federal police officers stood on the banks of a dirty river in the hot sun and watched some bare-chested men pull a badly decomposed human leg from a bush where it had snagged.

"That seems to be more of him," one of the officers muttered. The dismembered leg belonged to a well-known drug dealer, a man who had made his living in the local marijuana and cocaine-shopping trade since the 1970s, but who had lately run into some trouble from the outside gang of bloodthirsty brutes from Mexico City who had moved up to the border to claim the business for themselves. For several days now, body parts of the local drug dealer had been turning up at various places along the river.

The police knew that ritual mutilations were a trademark of the Mexico City gang. Dismembered bodies often came floating down the river, usually with the spines ripped out. This is the way the ancient Aztecs prepared humans for sacrifice—ripping out the spines.

The federal officer watched the men on the riverbank and then looked without emotion at his partner. They both knew who was responsible.

"El Padrino," the officer said.

Adolfo de Jesus Constanzo was a deadly serious young man, born in Miami in 1962, to a mother who was fifteen years old, divorced already, and just off a boat from Cuba.

A good-looking boy with dark eyes and light skin, he grew up a fussy and apprehensive child who was afraid to get his clothes dirty and always stayed close to his mother. His meticulousness was remarkable, considering he grew up in a small apartment where his mother kept an altar in the living room on which she displayed ceramic busts of saints and sacrificed live chickens and the occasional baby goat, as part of her voodoolike Santeria religious devotions. Beside that altar was a companion shrine, just a little smaller, which his mother had devoted to another icon, Marilyn Monroe.

At the same time, she insisted that little Adolfo present to the outside world a respectable middle-class picture of upward mobility. At her urging, he became a Roman Catholic altar boy, getting up at dawn to pick his way through the goats and chickens in the yard to make his way to church carrying his neatly pressed cassock. She boasted that he was going to be a doctor and live with the rich in Boca Raton when he grew up.

Small wonder that the boy began experiencing visions by the onset of adolescence. At the age of fourteen the intense Adolfo held his mother spellbound with his description of a startling spiritual experience: Marilyn Monroe herself had appeared to him to tell him that she had not committed suicide. She had died of natural causes! His mother was fascinated by the boy's supernatural powers. Eventually, he dropped out of high school to pursue them.

There was a job market for mystics in the Miami of Adolfo's youth. As hundreds of thousands of immigrants from the Caribbean poured into southern Florida during the 1970s, many brought with them a religious culture in which a Roman Catholic facade had been constructed over a foundation based on African-Caribbean spiritual beliefs in the worship of ancient gods who must be appeased with various offerings. *Botánicas*—stores that sell herbs, religious statues, candles, and other supplies for these occult practices—sprang up like delis all over immigrant neighborhoods of South Florida. The greater the favor, bigger the problem, or darker the vendetta, the larger the offering. In a *botánica* one can also hire practitioners who cast spells, summon spirits, exorcise demons, and cure sicknesses.

After working a series of odd jobs and shoplifting to buy drugs, Adolfo began to make a living as such a person, casting spells in storefront *botánicas*. After an apprenticeship, his reputation began to grow; as his clientele expanded, he became more deeply immersed in the murkier occult world where everyday Santeria crosses the line into the deeply demonic, black-magic dark side of Santeria, *palo mayombe,* a belief devoted to evil and obsessed with threats, greed, violence, and bloodshed. Those who have studied *palo mayombe* maintain that it attracts the worst elements in society. As such, it is the perfect religion for the drug trade.

The secret priests of the cult, called *mayomberos,* preside over rituals that employ witches' caldrons into which a gory stew of ingredients—often including human remains, sometimes dug up from graves —are assembled for offering to voodoo gods. Santeros cleanly kill their animal sacrifices, avoiding unnecessary pain. To *mayomberos,* torture and pain are inherent to the ritual. At its most extreme, *palo mayombe* ritual uses live humans.

The streets where this violent spiritual world displays its wares are the same ones from which the most violent manifestations of the brutal new Caribbean drug culture transformed South Florida life in the 1970s. By the time he was eighteen, Adolfo swaggered along those streets with a sense of entitlement, radiating menace. *Mayomberos* dealt with enemies through evil spells; drug dealers had more direct methods. Having a foot in both worlds, Adolfo sensed a certain symbiosis in combining the two.

Still, competition was fierce. Drug dealers—even those claiming spiritual gifts—were in abundant supply in Miami; gunfire had become a common part of the business day. Adolfo had more visions. In one of them he saw the future for a smart, urbane entrepreneur, fluent in Spanish, such as himself: Mexico City.

Not that the Mexico City that Adolfo moved to in 1980 had any great need for another small-time drug dealer with big plans and a gun in his pocket. It had thousands of those, with hungry new recruits to the drug trade pouring in every day from South America and the Caribbean. Breaking into that business didn't require brains—it required raw courage.

With plenty of the former and none of the latter, Adolfo assessed the situation through an instinctive grasp of market forces that would have served him well in any business he entered. Beneath its cosmopolitan veneer as a world-class city, Mexico City harbors a darkly superstitious indigenous culture, where spirits and magic run as major subcurrents just below the surface of everyday life. Even well-to-do, educated citizens routinely seek advice or purchase spells—to ensure good luck, repel bad luck, or even invoke harm on enemies—from seers and storefront witches.

With his expertise in selling both sorcery and drugs, Adolfo decided he could make his fortune in such a place. To the indigenous Mexican superstitions of Brujeria, which has Aztec roots and concerns itself with witchcraft and herbal healing, maternal security and stern justice, he added the dark and frightening elements of *palo mayombe,* and opened for business. Realizing that the high end of the market was underserved, as street crime discouraged more affluent citizens from seeking out witches in run-down neighborhoods, Adolfo set himself up in a luxury office like a doctor, and waited for the carriage trade to come.

"Welcome to the house of the devil," he would intone as affluent clients, some of them recruited in gay bars or flashy singles nightclubs, walked nervously through the door with their money in hand.

This ability to move with ease through the capital's expensive and cliquish nightclubs had been honed well in South Florida, where Adolfo—unable to maintain close relationships with anyone except his mother—had for years prowled the anonymous leather bars and pickup joints of the Florida Gold Coast, moving from one temporarily intense homosexual relationship to another.

"He seemed to prefer men who were mirror images of himself: handsome, smooth, and nicely dressed. He treated his lovers well, showering them with generous gifts and writing passionate love letters and poems," author Cliff Linedecker wrote in *Hell Ranch,* a 1989 book about the Constanzo drug cult.

As the money came in, Adolfo dressed the part and refined his act, sometimes moving with an expensive and stunning companion—male or female—on his arm, always moving with the flow of cocaine, hash, and boutique drugs by the handful.

Everything was business, day and night. In a short time Adolfo numbered among his clients well-known movie and television performers and business and government figures, who might bump with drug kingpins, transvestites, or street thugs in his outer office. All of them seemed to be afraid of something or someone, and many, he realized, had good reason for their anxiety. He was in a position to help. As the layers of clients and supplicants piled up in growing complexity, the services he could offer multiplied as well. With police officers and politicians in his fold, the spiritual protection he could offer through rituals took on aspects of political and criminal protection as well. Money, drugs, guns, and spirits all flowed through this rapacious network of contacts. There was a certain logic in purchasing spiritual protection from a *mayombero* who associated with so many violent thugs and knew so many people with influence. It all interlocked.

For a price—determined by exactly what he wanted at the time—anyone could be protected from evil within a magical shield of blood that Adolfo could cause to envelope them. Even an enemy could be made to die. Adolfo personally knew the very people who could arrange it.

In 1985, after a devastating earthquake killed thousands and rocked Mexico City's corrupt aristocracy to its social foundations, Adolfo spread the rumor through his networks that he had predicted the quake. By now Adolfo had a villa and a downtown apartment. Traveling in the ostentatious style that only a drug kingpin can affect, constantly surrounded by an entourage, he even made several noisy trips home to South Florida to see his mother and show her what a personage he had become. Everywhere he traveled, drug deals trailed along.

Ultimately, Adolfo's path led to the northern Mexican border town of Matamoros, hard by the Texas city of Brownsville. Given its geography, Matamoros is a logical transshipment point for smugglers looking for the closest gateway to the key importing operations run by the Chicago Mafia. As such, it is one of the half-dozen most important smuggling channels into America. In such a place, drug money and its corrupting influence not only pervades all layers of daily life, it almost defines that life. Fear of official intimidation coexists with the fear of criminal retribution—on the street, in the courts and municipal offices, in the home, in commerce and industry.

Here, it is said, one does not demand justice. One bargains for it.

This atmosphere often seeps slowly across the border, where violent crime rates have skyrocketed in South Texas towns. U.S. law enforcement officials and customs agents have become deeply frustrated by the flagrant corruption they encounter among their counterparts in border boomtowns like Matamoros, where drug lords flashing diamond-studded Rolex watches swagger openly like princes, commuting to town by helicopter from seaside mansions. These criminal overlords support a virtual welfare state of functionaries, layered downward from corrupt officials who provide protection to battalions of young boys who work as "mules," smuggling and distributing the contraband. Kidnapping, torture, murder, and assassination are routine occurrences. Poorly paid, badly trained, and barely supervised, Mexican federal police officers often are regarded as little more than badge-carrying assassins. Worse, law enforcement standards are so abysmal that drug kingpins routinely manage to obtain badges and appointments to the police force for whomever they designate.

"Federal narcotics police are accountable for a large number of the cases of murder, torture, and abuse of due process in Mexico today," the international human-rights group Americas Watch declared in a 1990 report, which found that Mexico's federal officers "routinely commit criminal acts far worse than those they are trying to stop."

But at least that was business, murderous as it was. In recent years an influx of ruthless Central American thugs has brought an even more frightening complication into the mix—an overlay of magic, superstition, and demonic ritualism.

"We see more Cubans and Colombians infiltrating the drug trade, either working with old-line Mexican drug families or taking over," one U.S. narcotics agent said about the intensifying problems coming from towns like Matamoros during the second half of the 1980s. Members of these new gangs sometimes came from cultures where occult religious practices were an integral aspect of criminal life. "As they come in, they're bringing this supernatural stuff with them," said the agent. The old rules no longer applied. Violent criminals were problem enough, but at least they feared a bullet. Criminals who believe they have a pact with the devil—a pact that ensures them eternal life—are a cop's worst nightmare.

Such a man—moving in a big way into the Matamoros drug scene in the late eighties—was Adolfo de Jesus Constanzo. By 1987, Adolfo was a well-known sight in Matamoros, a swaggering *mayombero* who prowled the gay whorehouses of the Boy's Town district by night, set up a protection racket by day, and traveled to and from Mexico City in a new Mercedes with a driver.

Besides being adjacent to the spring break party town of South Padre Island, Matamoros's U.S. neighbor, Brownsville, is the site of Texas Southmost College, an institution that attracts a large number of students from Mexico. This is where, late in 1987 while on an informal mission to recruit new followers, Adolfo met the beautiful Sara Maria Aldrette Villarreal, a tall and slender twenty-three-year-old Mexican student who fell immediately under his influence. Sara saw Adolfo as handsome, accomplished, and, most of all, rich enough to satisfy her expensive whims.

He saw her as a necessary final ingredient for his plan to take over the Matamoros drug-smuggling operations. Sara had a brief love affair with Constanzo, whose homosexual preferences were well-known to everyone who knew him intimately—except his mother in South Florida. Adolfo's mother, in fact, was the main reason for the sexual affair with Sara. He brought the statuesque beauty home to his mother in her now well-furnished apartment, which still had the Santeria altar beside the one to Marilyn Monroe.

"Mommy, this is the girl I am going to marry," he said proudly, having no intention of doing anything other than pleasing his mother with a fantasy before going back to business in Mexico City.

"Very beautiful," she said appraisingly. "She is a Mexican?"

Adolfo and Sara went back to his villa outside of Mexico City for a few weeks. By the time they returned to Matamoros, the affair was over. But Sara had graduated to a much more important role in his scheme—she became his high priestess, the necessary female acolyte in the dark rituals of *palo mayombe*.

With Sara at his side, Constanzo moved easily as he quietly recruited followers in the northern Mexico border towns, where the flashy Cuban from Mexico City had to contend with a suspicious and deeply machismo local drug culture. This entrée was important because a deeply entrenched Mexican drug organization, the Hernandez gang, already controlled the business in the Matamoros region and had no intention of yielding ground. From its distribution center at the isolated Rancho Santa Elena, south of Matamoros, the Hernandez gang moved thousands of pounds of marijuana and quantities of cocaine each week through its long-established contacts in U.S. crime organizations north of the border.

But the Hernandez group was being torn apart by bloody gang warfare when Adolfo arrived on the scene, and he adroitly manipulated the warring factions to his own use. As he had in Mexico City, he offered protection from harm. Again, he depended on a well-paid network of corrupt officials, a cadre of gun-toting thugs, and a surfeit of magical spiritualism to accomplish the task.

Sara herself brought in one of the major figures in a warring faction of the Hernandez gang, a quick-tempered Matamoros strong-arm specialist, twenty-two-year-old Alvaro de Leon Valdez, whose nickname was El Duby.

Adolfo and Sara recruited him like a hot job prospect in the corporate world. They introduced him to the other major members of the organization. They wined him and dined him. And in the Mercedes, they drove him to Mexico City to spend a few days at Adolfo's villa. It was an sprawling hacienda, with a pool and a tennis court, a house framed with palms and surrounded by a fence with a great iron gate. The neighbors were lawyers, government officials, and *federales*.

Adolfo tried to explain the interlocking spiritual and the financial aspects of the business to El Duby. He and his cohorts had capital, influence, firepower —and access to the major Colombian and other

South American manufacturing operations that were
revolutionizing the drug business and driving the
Mexicans out of their own trade. What they needed
was the solid inroad that El Duby would provide into
the Hernandez operation. With El Duby on board, it
would only be a matter of time before the entire
operation would fall to Adolfo's control.

Adolfo was very persuasive.

"Listen, you can stay where you are and get killed
with those fucking greasers," he said, "or you can
come with me and live forever, and live with class."

El Duby looked at the beautiful Sara. His eyes
roamed over the luxurious, sun-splashed, white-
washed rooms of the villa. He did not need any more
time to think about it.

"I'm with you, man," he said.

Within a month Adolfo had established himself as
the kingpin of the border smuggling operation. He
did this through the usual blend of mysticism and
terror—the dismembered bodies with their spines
severed were one graphic calling card. Adolfo used
Sara, El Duby, and others in a brilliant campaign of
psychological warfare that convinced many of the
warring gang members of the wisdom of enlisting in
the temporal and spiritual protection ring that he
offered. Everybody would make a lot more money—
and, they said, live forever—once they joined up.
Adolfo even obtained a Mexican Federal Judicial Police badge. Among his close friends, it was known,
was Commander Florentino Ventura Gutierrez, the
man who headed the federal police.

Before long the Hernandez gang did not exist. In
its place, indeed operating with impunity from the

old Hernandez hideaway at Rancho Santa Elena, was a bloodthirsty drug cult that answered to one man, a man whose name was now just whispered: El Padrino.

Adolfo used the hideaway for the *palo mayombe*–influenced rituals that served to hold his gang together in spiritual bondage. From the ranch more than a ton of marijuana was baled and shipped north each week. The ranch also was used to cut and package shipments of cocaine bound for America. And when the work was done, the cult assembled there for the demonic rituals led by Adolfo. With Sara at his side as priestess, he drew "magical shields" in blood around gang members, offering them protection from all harm, even bullets. At first the rituals were based on animal sacrifices. But very quickly this changed. Human blood was needed, Adolfo said, for the magical shield to continue working. By now the cult had about three dozen regular members. Its core was a group of thugs led by El Duby, whose loyalty to El Padrino was unquestioned.

In 1989 a young man from a nearby village hitchhiking to a bus station along the Rio Grande was given a ride by two of Adolfo's men. He never was seen alive again. At the ranch, he was ceremoniously slaughtered and his blood drained into a witch's caldron.

He was buried in a grave on the ranch, the first of many to come. Soon afterward, young men and boys began vanishing from Matamoros and the small towns near the Rio Grande.

Though conceding her association with Adolfo, Sara would later steadfastly deny ever taking part in any of the human sacrifices. "It was like hell," she would claim about her life in the Constanzo drug cult, maintaining that she was a victim, not a perpetrator of the horrors. "They treated me like a prisoner. I don't know how I got into this without knowing what it was." Sara insisted that she followed Adolfo's orders because he threatened to harm her family with his witchcraft.

But some members would later claim that she was called La Madrina, the Godmother, and her name was whispered in the same hushed tones as that of El Padrino.

The name was no longer whispered after a day in April of 1989, one month after the disappearance of Mark Kilroy. A task force of special anticorruption Mexican police on routine drug-interdiction patrol in the Matamoros region chanced upon a suspicious pickup truck bouncing on the rutted coastal road in the barren scrubland where armadillos roamed and skinny cattle sagged in the heat, thirteen miles south of Matamoros.

They gave chase, following the pickup up a dirt road in a cloud of dust before the truck ran off the road into a ditch. Just beyond was a small collection of run-down clapboard buildings. The police followed the fleeing men into a small tin-roofed warehouse. Inside they encountered five men in all, along with the remnants of a big marijuana shipment and some odd statues and implements that the cops initially did not have time to study, since they were expecting armed resistance. But there was no gunfire.

The officers were baffled by the nonchalant way

the suspects stood there, unarmed, facing them. One of them was even giggling.

"What's the matter with you?" asked one of the cops. "Don't you know you're going to prison?"

"You will never take me," the man said. "Your bullets will bounce off."

"Why is that?"

"Because I am invisible. Around me is a magic shield."

The fallacy of this assertion was demonstrated when the arresting officers roughly slapped handcuffs on the suspects and pushed them into a corner, where their predicament sank in and they cowered as the police began to inspect the scene of horror inside the shack.

The stink of the place repulsed them, but not nearly as much as what they encountered inside. Beside the door, crawling with flies and maggots, was a great cast-iron pot, a veritable witch's caldron inside which was a congealed soup of repulsive liquid in which could be seen a horseshoe, a boiled turtle, a stump of a goat's foot, and, one of the officers realized with a surge of nausea, what appeared to be pieces of rotted of human flesh and brain matter.

Arrayed on one shelf were garishly painted statues of saints, the icons of *palo mayómbe*. Beside them were candle stumps, ceramic bowls caked with blood, and empty bottles. The plank floor was strewn with cigar butts, tequila bottles, a rotted goat's head, rusty wire hangers. In a corner was what appeared to be a bird's nest that, on closer inspection, seemed to be made of human hair. A blood-caked machete lay nearby.

The arresting officers called for additional assistance, not knowing what more they might encounter on the isolated ranch. Within a short time Mexican reinforcements arrived at the ranch, along with American agents working on the case.

By now the cultists' faith in their supernatural invulnerability had entirely disintegrated and they were ready to answer any question they were asked. "These guys caved in like cheap suitcases," one American agent said. They began to name names.

Among the reinforcements who arrived at the ranch were Oran Neck, the U.S. customs agent who had been helping Mark Kilroy's parents lead the search for their son. Neck always carried one of the missing persons flyers with Mark's picture on it, and he took it out and showed it to the men at the ranch, asking, "Have you seen this boy?"

"Yes," whimpered one of the men. "He is out there."

Outside, in a corral surrounded by a sagging wood fence, they found the crudely dug graves. The horrified arresting officers discovered twelve bodies under a few inches of dirt. All had been beheaded. One of them was a police informer who had disappeared while on a drug investigation. Others were young men who merely had the misfortune of being noticed by El Padrino, who would simply point them out at random on a street and tell his henchmen, "That one."

Then they dug up the remains of Mark Kilroy.

One of the men now in custody, Serafin Hernandez Garcia, who had been introduced to the cult by Sara Aldrette, explained that the American college boy had been kidnapped near the customs plaza at the border. The young man—chosen at random because El Padrino had decreed that a blond-haired Anglo male was required for a human sacrifice—had merely looked up and turned when he was approached by two emissaries of the cult. In a flash they pushed him into a car and drove off to the ranch, where he was bound. The next day he was led into the shed. The last thing Mark Kilroy saw before a machete hacked off his head was the face of a man dressed in a ceremonial white robe, smiling serenely in the flickering yellow glow of candlelight.

"Who made this sacrifice?" a cop demanded.

"El Padrino."

"We killed them for protection," another of the men in the cult, Elio Hernandez Rivera, twenty-two years old, explained.

At the police station, as the men were interrogated further, El Padrino was identified as Adolfo de Jesus Constanzo. They also gave the name of Sara Aldrette. "She is the witch," one of the men explained casually.

What's more, there were two addresses, one an apartment in Mexico City, the other a villa outside of the capital.

After learning about the raid on the ranch, Adolfo and Sara had fled Matamoros in his $60,000 Mercedes. By now there was no talk of any magic shield. Instead, El Padrino found a phone to call his mother in Miami and wail that he was being persecuted by the corrupt police, but he had done nothing wrong.

"Mommy, do not believe the terrible things you will see on television!" he sobbed.

As he made this plea to his mother, Mexican police were raiding his home in Matamoros. At the same time, the *federales* had arrived with machine guns at his empty villa outside Mexico City. Inside they discovered ritualistic altars and the other claptrap of the occult paranoia, along with the accoutrements of a fine entrepreneurial life such as thousand-dollar suits, diamond jewelry, and gold watches.

"He was a fine neighbor," said a man who lived down the street. "No trouble."

In the Mercedes, Adolfo and Sara hurtled south across the mountains. They arrived at the apartment in Mexico City, where El Duby had been staying while working on a business deal. Like Adolfo, El Duby saw himself as a debonair figure. His nickname, in fact, was owed to his nervous habit of crooning the Frank Sinatra lyric "dooby-dooby-do" as he worked.

Ever loyal, El Duby welcomed El Padrino and Sara into the apartment and said they would be safe.

But shortly after they got there, Adolfo had another vision: the police were coming. This vision turned out to be entirely correct.

An hour later, when the wail of sirens rose up from the street, Adolfo grabbed a gun and went berserk for fear of being taken away in disgrace like a common criminal.

"They're here! Why run? Don't hide!" he shrieked.

"He went crazy, crazy," El Duby later recalled. "He began shooting out the window. He said everything, everything, was lost. He said, 'No one is going to have this money!'"

So Adolfo threw the money out the fourth-floor window onto the police rushing the entrance of the building. Neighbors hurried out to try to snatch up bills that sifted down like so much confetti.

In the apartment, while Sara cried, Adolfo slapped El Duby in the face and then ordered El Duby to kill him, "because it is the end and I want to die."

El Duby raised his machine gun. As always, he did as he was told.

CHAPTER EIGHT

Yahweh

HE CALLED HIMSELF the son of God. Yahweh Ben Yahweh was not a modest man.

"Egypt has the pyramids," the towering black religious leader declared in a 1990 speech to a gathering of admiring South Florida business executives. "India has the Taj Mahal. France has the Eiffel Tower. Rome has the Pope. Orlando has Disney. Miami has the son of Yahweh.

"The world's greatest attraction is in your midst," he said. "I'm here."

He is now in prison, but before his time ran out, Yahweh had quite a run in South Florida. For many years his male followers, known as "Yahwehs," were familiar figures in Miami, steely-eyed men dressed completely in white, with turbans on their heads. In *Esquire* magazine the writer Pete Hamill recalled covering the Miami riots in 1989 and encountering a quartet of burly Yahwehs who looked "like the house band from one of those velvet-roped mob joints with names like the Oasis or the Aladdin." Hamill described Yahweh's real name, Hulon Mitchell, Jr., as "a name right out of a Elmore Leonard novel."

But there wasn't anything amusing about the Yahwehs, despite their comic-opera costumes and banana-republic military deportment. To cross Yahwehs was to flirt with danger. A severed head was only one of the Yahwehs' grisly calling cards.

"I am the Messiah, I am the word. I am incarnate," Mitchell proclaimed in a 1986 interview with the *New York Times.*

But later he would argue that grandiose claims of omnipotence aside, he wasn't really aware of what was going on. The murders, mutilations, beatings, firebombings, and extortions all had been done without his knowledge, the son of God would insist.

Until they were finally brought down by federal prosecutors, Yahweh and hundreds of his followers ran a criminal enterprise under cover of the Nation of Yahweh, a religious sect headquartered in a former supermarket that had been burned and looted in the 1980 Liberty City riots in Miami. They called the headquarters the Temple of Love, but it was really a den of inequity.

For over a decade the Temple was a politically potent, well-organized community force that depended on business acumen and well-orchestrated publicity to cover up the truth about its real activities.

Actually, law enforcement authorities and others suspected the truth almost from the beginning. In 1981, just two years after Yahweh founded the Temple of Love, the first headless body turned up with what looked like Yahweh's imprint on the crime.

Joining Yahweh was regarded as a lifelong commitment, which is something the victim of that beheading, Aston Green, apparently forgot when he and two roommates decided to leave the sect that year, ignoring Yahweh's warning that "heads will roll" unless they returned to the fold. It turned out he meant it literally.

On November 12, according to court testimony many years later, ten Yahweh members took Green into a back room of the Temple of Love, beat him, bound and gagged him, wrapped him in a carpet and drove to a secluded area, where a machete was taken to him while he was still alive.

A jogger found Green in a field. His head turned up nearby.

Horrified, Green's roommates, postal worker Mildred Banks and accountant Carlton Carey, told police that they suspected the Yahwehs had executed Green in retaliation for leaving the sect. Shortly after they returned from the police station, the two roommates were slashed and shot in their North Dade home by two men wearing ski masks and brandishing guns and swords. Banks, who managed to crawl to a neighbor's house and call an ambulance, recovered from her wounds. Carey did not.

Detectives investigating the crimes found evidence at the Temple of Love, similar pieces of carpet, which seemed to implicate the Yahwehs. Yahweh and his chief deputy, a woman who had taken the name Judith Israel, refused to talk. So did everyone else. The case went nowhere.

A newspaper story at the time speculated on the

reason for the impotent investigation: Authorities were reluctant to be seen going after a black religious leader with an enthusiastic following, a man who courted politicians, who had been lionized in the media as a savior of the ghetto and a paragon of black community enterprise. Instead, the police waited and kept files.

"We always felt somewhere along the line someone would trip up and they'd start talking," an investigator said.

It would take almost another decade to bring Yahweh and his killer cult to justice.

The self-proclaimed messiah Yahweh Ben Yahweh was born Hulon Mitchell, Jr., in 1935 in Kingfisher, Oklahoma, the oldest of fifteen children. His father was a grainery laborer who worked weekends as a Pentecostal preacher. Mitchell and his brothers and sisters all sang in the church choir. Though they grew up in a poor, racially segregated environment, the children apparently gained some sense of life's possibilities. In fact, one of Hulon's sisters, Leona Mitchell, went on to become a featured soprano with the Metropolitan Opera.

For a time Hulon Mitchell looked as if he too was on the right track. After a hitch in the Air Force, he used the GI Bill to get a B.A. in psychology at Phillips College in Oklahoma, and even went on to law school at the University of Oklahoma. But he dropped out, moved to the Chicago suburbs, and became involved with the Black Muslim sect.

This is where he first changed his name—to Hulon Shah. But the blue-eyed firebrand was expelled from the Chicago sect because of his violent racial views.

Over the years, he would move frequently, often changing his name and religious identity. In Atlanta he turned up as Father Michel and had his own storefront church during the 1970s. There, he cobbled together a religious philosophy based on the theory that whites are the root of all evil. This he later imported to a new undertaking in the Liberty City neighborhood of Miami. Now calling himself Brother Moses, he wrote of the white race as "the devil, Satan, serpent, and beast," with special invective against Jews and the "synagogue of Satan."

Philosophically, the beliefs he brought to Miami were a hybrid offshoot of a black triumphalist sect founded in Detroit in 1930, which proclaimed that blacks, the original humans and true heirs to the Promised Land, have been persecuted throughout history by a bastard race of whites that sprang from a diabolical prehistoric breeding experiment. With their compelling appeal to black self-esteem and past cultural greatness, such claims are often heard on corner soapboxes from Times Square to Golden Gate Park.

But Brother Moses was no ordinary street hustler by the time he got to Miami. Claiming that he had died in his thirties and risen from the dead as messiah of the lost black tribe of Israel, the dapper charismatic renamed himself Yahweh Ben Yahweh—God the Son of God—and founded a new church, the Temple of Love, gathering hordes of new followers, who renovated the burned-out supermarket into a fortress.

The Yahwehs churned out publications and tapes to distribute their racist theories nationally. At the center of the enterprise, Yahweh himself was an imposing figure. Tall, turbaned, and bejeweled, invariably surrounded by white-robed bodyguards who carried six-foot wood staffs, Yahweh and his twin message of hope and retribution attracted not only poor and disenfranchised neighborhood residents, but also scores of young black professionals, including teachers and lawyers. It was a message that found especially fertile ground in poor black Miami neighborhoods, still enraged over the beating death of a black insurance executive by police officers in 1979.

The message was fairly simple, especially to people desperate for hope and overwhelmed by misery. White people were the root of all evil, the thieves of a long-lost nobility rightfully belonging to the black race. One of the first widely distributed Yahweh publications was titled, "You Are Not a Nigger. The World's Best-Kept Secret."

A typical follower was B'Ruraw Geela Israel, who grew up in Liberty City. After reading one of the Yahweh pamphlets handed to her on a street corner in 1984, she went to the Temple and heard the leader deliver his compelling message of individual responsibility and black pride.

"It blew my mind," she told the *Miami Herald.* "Some of us can truly see he is the son of God."

Another follower, Ruth Israel, recounted the first time she went to the Temple to hear Yahweh Ben Yahweh speak. "He came in and walked on stage. He was handsome. He spoke, and it just hit me. He started giving me the wisdom of the word and I said, 'This has to be it.' I had never heard anyone speak like this man before."

"When I read 'You Are Not a Nigger,' I knew he

had to be somebody divine," said another, Shalisha Israel. "The answers that he gave, the documentation he gave from the scripture . . .".

Perhaps the most important follower recruited by Yahweh was Judith Israel, a woman with a flair for business, who would become the leader's second-in-command and treasurer and, police said, common-law wife. Her real name was Linda Gaines, and she met Yahweh in Orlando during the late 1970s, when he was still calling himself Brother Moses. She was in charge of the sect's nonreligious activities, especially its finances.

Outwardly, the Temple of Love was a model of initiative and self-sufficient resourcefulness. The complex was neat, scrubbed, and well-maintained. Like Black Muslims, Yahweh members eliminated their "slave names." Yahwehs adopted the last name Israel.

Except for the assertive Judith Israel, whose position as Yahweh's aide-de-camp was unassailable, women were expected to stay in the background and remain silent. Raising money through panhandling and street vending was their major duty.

When they weren't fanning out through the community to solicit donations and proselytize for new members, Yahwehs were expected to lead a monastic life at the Temple, where a fearsome squad of elite guard known as the Circle of Ten rigidly enforced discipline. Many of the women—and some girls as young as fourteen—were expected to provide sexual services to Yahweh.

The Yahwehs established an impressive business record in Miami. In the entrepreneurial spirit of the

1980s, they rehabilitated crack houses as residences for sect members. Under Judith Israel's direction, they deftly acquired minority-enterprise loans and government contracts. They opened shops, a beauty salon, even an elementary school called Yahweh University, where children paid strict attention and chanted their lessons for admiring visitors.

By the end of the decade the Temple of Love's holdings would include twenty-six properties worth about $9 million, and the group was claiming to have more than 10,000 members.

Like the Move cult in Philadelphia, the Yahwehs delivered their own babies, since the leader forbade the use of hospitals for childbirth. Several infants who died during birth were buried on the Temple grounds, followers later said.

As the sect prospered, Yahweh kept up a steady drumbeat of invective against dissidents and defectors.

Neighbors who complained about noise and threats, or who ran afoul of Yahweh street organizers, quickly learned not to call the police.

The long-dormant criminal investigation into the Yahwehs stirred back to life in the mid-eighties. Police interviewed numerous defectors who told them of a public execution of a Yahweh that had taken place in the Temple in 1983.

The victim, a twenty-two-year-old national karate champion named Leonard Dupree, had been beaten to death inside the Temple after becoming involved in an argument with a woman member. After Dupree was beaten, police were told, sect members kicked him to death while Yahweh watched.

Thirty to fifty disciples set upon Dupree, some using clubs and a tire iron. The body was loaded into a truck and buried in the Everglades, authorities were later told.

Though they had witnesses who claimed to have seen the attack, police had no corpse. Prosecutors decided there was not enough evidence for any criminal indictments.

But the investigators' case files kept growing.

In May of 1986, after a group of Yahweh solicitors were roughed up by drug dealers, sect members stormed the block and firebombed several homes.

"Yahweh took vengeance on his enemy," a participant would later testify.

"I heard people screaming," sect member Neariah Israel, one of the participants who threw Molotov cocktails, would recall. "I lit another one."

Later that year Yahweh named Neariah Israel as a "death angel" charged with killing enemies of the sect. It would be the biggest mistake of Yahweh's life.

Quietly, the FBI joined the case in the aftermath of the firebombing. For a brief time anti-Yahweh publicity flared on the still-unproved reports of the sect's involvement in the firebombings.

"They are a hate group," Willie Simms, a member of the Dade County Community Relations Board, said in 1986. "These people are brainwashed. I fear for the city."

Another violent outbreak was laid to the Yahwehs in late 1986. As part of its aggressive business expansion, the sect purchased a rat-infested apartment complex in the poor Miami suburb of Opa-Locka.

The hundred existing tenants, all blacks, were ordered to vacate their apartments. But some refused.

In October, a seventy-five-man Yahweh eviction squad rolled up to the building in two limousines, six buses, and several cars. In their white robes and sandals, the menacing Yahwehs piled out with their six-foot clubs and surrounded the building.

Two men who resisted being evicted from their apartments were shot, beaten to death, and then beheaded.

Police immediately arrested a man found hiding near the complex and charged him in the murders. The suspect gave his name as Neariah Israel and said that he was 404 years old.

But his real identity created quite a stir when it became known. The thirty-three-year-old Neariah Israel was actually Robert Ernest Rozier Jr., a former defensive end for the St. Louis Cardinals and Oakland Raiders in the seventies. He had joined the sect after turning over his bank account and other holdings.

Rozier was the man who would bring down the empire.

Yahweh made the mistake of taxing Rozier's loyalty by letting him stew unhappily in jail. After seven months Rozier angrily demanded that Yahweh provide him with a new lawyer. The request did not sit well with the son of God, who denounced Rozier as a "black devil" and presided over a public ceremony at the Temple of Love in which Rozier was excommunicated from the sect.

Police and prosecutors worked for over a year to leverage this rift and engineer a deal with Rozier, who in 1988 finally pleaded guilty to participating in four murders for the Yahwehs. In exchange for the plea and for agreeing to give detailed evidence against the Yahwehs, Rozier was able to avoid the electric chair and receive a twenty-two-year prison sentence instead.

Soon after Rozier started talking, the rumors took on graphic dimensions. Crimes like the Opa-Locka killings were clearly the work of the Yahwehs, but authorities were astonished at the story Rozier told of widespread murder, retribution, and greed.

Rozier implicated the Yahwehs in a number of unsolved murders that had perplexed Miami police for years. He also described how Yahweh controlled members of his inner circle, the security force known as the "Brotherhood," with demands that they provide grisly proof of their devotion.

"Kill me a white devil and bring me an ear," Yahweh ordered, according to Rozier.

Police shuddered at hearing that. In the mid-eighties, eight white vagrants had been found murdered, with their ears cut off, in alleys and other places throughout Miami. Until Rozier told them that the vagrants had been chosen at random and murdered by himself and other Yahwehs, authorities had suspected the mutilation killings were the work of a single deranged serial killer.

Yahweh, who insisted on seeing proof of the kill, liked to carry the ears around and often showed them to people for fun. Prosecutors later obtained testimony from more than fifty other witnesses who corroborated Rozier's accounts.

One follower recalled Yahweh taking an ear out of

a brown-paper lunch bag and displaying it with a grin.

"See this hairy devil!" Yahweh said.

"Praise Yahweh," the follower replied uneasily.

For Rozier and certain members of the Brotherhood, the ears were the price of admission.

While Rozier was in jail after the firebombings of 1986, the Nation of Yahweh changed course, curtailed its violence and toned down the racist rhetoric. It redoubled its efforts to establish black-owned businesses in poor areas of Miami and South Florida. The Nation even enrolled in the Chamber of Commerce.

Diligently courting politicians and business leaders in much the way Jim Jones had done more than a decade earlier in San Francisco, Yahweh managed to transform the image of his followers from menace to virtue. The Nation of Yahweh and its Temple of Love established antidrug programs. Under the guidance of Judith Israel, the Temple's coffers filled and its real estate holdings grew.

In their flowing robes and turbans, Yahwehs became familiar sights at political rallies and community meetings and were especially active in voter registration drives. Under Judith Israel's direction, the group's rapidly expanding business holdings encompassed a $9 million portfolio of well-tended apartment complexes, motels, strip malls, bakeries, warehouses, and other businesses. Among them was a grocery store given rent-free to the Yahwehs by the city of Miami, whose taxpayers funded $300,000 worth of equipment and renovations.

Yahweh became an emblem of successful black enterprise. Drawn by the impression of black political power, local, county, and state politicians were eager to be seen at his Temple and receive Yahweh's endorsement—since it was clear that Yahweh's followers voted the way they were told. Visiting dignitaries were always videotaped by Temple publicists. The videos were used for promotion and fund-raising purposes.

Still, as with Jones's People's Temple in San Francisco, disturbing rumors about abuses in the Nation of Yahweh were never far below the surface—for anyone who cared to look for them. To many black residents, the name Yahweh was always associated with violence, intimidation, and terror, no matter what the Yahweh public relations machine said. Furthermore, Dade County child-welfare authorities had been hearing reports about the abuse of children at the Temple for years.

The Yahwehs' blatantly racist antiwhite literature left no room for ambiguity. Moreover, the sect published paranoiac tracts that sounded eerily reminiscent of Jim Jones and his Temple. "We have come to the point where we must find justice for ourselves or commit suicide," one Yahweh publication said. "Suicide" and "race riot" were common terms in Yahweh's writings.

Yet the political acclaim persisted even after Yahweh's name had been publicly connected to murder and other criminal activities. For example, in October of 1990—four months after the *Miami Herald* published startling allegations linking the Yahwehs to murders and other violent crimes—Miami Mayor Xavier Suarez issued an official proclamation making October 7 "Yahweh Ben Yahweh Day." Writing later in *Esquire* magazine, Pete Hamill noted the irony of this act: "Miami, after all, was the only city in the country that refused to honor Nelson Mandela during his American tour."

. Yahweh's honors did not last much longer, however.

It had taken too many years to put the case together. Law enforcement officials would later privately concede that worries about the appearance of racial or religious prejudice in prosecuting a successful black community enterprise were partly responsible for the slow pace of the investigation, which was handled by the U.S. Attorney's office as the result of an agreement with the state. But by the autumn of 1990, federal prosecutors felt they were finally ready with a solid case. On November 7, 1990, Yahweh and fifteen of his followers were charged with conspiracy and racketeering in what U.S. Attorney Dexter Lehtinen called a "reign of terror" masterminded by Yahweh Ben Yahweh throughout South Florida. Lehtinen called the Yahwehs a "cult" and said the indictments had ended an "era of extreme violence . . .

"The defendants engaged in violence as a mechanism for keeping discipline, and violence as a mechanism for making money," Lehtinen said. "Yahweh Ben Yahweh trusted no one," the prosecutor said—not even those who killed on his orders. "He made them bring back parts of the body."

The indictment accused the group of killing fourteen people, including former members who displeased Yahweh with disloyalty or "blasphemy," and of terroristic activities such as the neighborhood firebombing. Among those indicted was Judith Israel. The indictment called her the "financial brains" of the operation.

The indictment also made note of the plight of children in the cult, and charged that Yahweh "exercised control by separating families of followers within the enterprise, by regulating the personal and sexual lives of married followers and by having sexual relations with both adult and minor female followers."

Yahweh was on business in New Orleans when the indictment was handed up. FBI agents had already staked out the French Quarter hotel where he was staying in an expensive suite, accompanied by several bodyguards. The phone in that suite rang at five A.M. on the morning of the indictment. The leader himself answered.

"FBI," he was told. "We have a warrant for your arrest."

About thirty-five FBI agents were waiting for him in the lobby. Wearing his white robe and turban, Yahweh was taken away in handcuffs.

As soon as Yahweh was in custody, word was flashed to agents and local cops in seven states, who had staked out locations of others named in the indictment. They sprang into action in precision raids.

In Miami more than fifty FBI agents and local police SWAT units moved on the block-long Temple of Love complex at 2766 NW 62nd Street, using a battering ram to break down the door.

Judith Israel was arrested in Atlanta at the same time. Other defendants were nabbed in raids the same day in North Carolina and Lafayette, Louisiana. In all, thirteen of the people named in the indictments were in custody within minutes of Yahweh's arrest.

In the bail hearing after the arrest, Yahweh identified himself as "the first begotten son of God."

Responding to the arrests, the Nation of Yahweh intensified its public-relations campaign. Some newspaper ads commissioned by Yahweh cited various cold weather spells, floods, hurricanes, disease epidemics, and even locust plagues as the result of Yahweh's arrest. Other printed and broadcast ads relentlessly reiterated the theme that Yahweh was being persecuted because of his race and religion.

Yahweh's defense attorney was Alcee L. Hastings, a former federal judge who was impeached by Congress in 1989 amid accusations of bribery, a charge on which he was later acquitted. Calling the government's case against his client a "travesty of justice," Hastings said the persecution of Yahweh should be a warning: "If they can indict this religion they can go after any religion." During the trial, he described his client as a "Gandhiesque" figure persecuted for his good works among the poor.

Rozier was the prosecution's star witness, but sixty-three others also testified, including a dozen former followers, many of whom had eyewitness accounts of murder and mayhem ordered by Yahweh.

For his part, Yahweh insisted that he was innocent of murder. He maintained that he found out about the murders only after followers came to him and confessed their sins, although he did describe himself in court as the "Grand Master of the Celestial Lodge, Architect of the Universe and Only Potentate and Founder of the Nation of Yahweh."

He said, "They were telling me about it after they had done it," and compared himself to a priest bound by the confidentiality of confession. Yahweh also said that the 1986 firebombing in Delray Beach was solely the work of renegade members of the sect, led by Rozier, whom he called a "serial killer."

In a television interview during the trial he said that "one or two people got together on their own" to cut the head off one victim. Yahweh cast himself as a man betrayed even by his own sister, Jean Solomon, who had testified that he watched the beating and execution of Leonard Dupree, and then ordered followers to pummel the dead man's body.

"The man called Christ had many false witnesses against him," Yahweh lamented. "It's a racist trial," he said, venturing a prediction on the outcome: "I expect, absolutely, divine intervention."

It didn't work out that way.

After hearing four months of testimony, the jury convicted Yahweh and six followers—including Linda Gaines—of conspiracy, including the commission of murders. Seven other followers were acquitted; the jury deadlocked on two others. The jury acquitted or was hung as to all the racketeering charges.

In September 1992, U.S. District Judge Norman Roettger shocked prosecutors by giving Yahweh eighteen years in prison—two years less than the maximum sentence. The judge maintained that Yahweh's community work warranted some consideration.

Assistant U.S. Attorney Richard Scruggs protested: "Judge, there are literally hundreds of victims in this case. Some died in pain, others will have to live in pain. This man is a classic con man, a classic megalomaniac. This is a man who used religion as a shield to amass power and money and commit horrendous crimes."

The judge conceded, "From the evidence I heard, the crimes were so horrendous, so gross, that the maximum twenty-year sentence is simply not commensurate with the crimes." But he noted the sect's record in establishing grocery stores, hotels, and apartment complexes in poor neighborhoods. "I think that deserves some reward," Roettger said. "The Nation of Yahweh, under the direction of the defendant, cleaned up its act—or acts—and tried to be a good citizen."

During the trial, Rozier—who had already pleaded guilty to four murders and was serving his sentence in a federal prison under a new identity—admitted that he actually killed six people on behalf of his leader. "As an order coming from Yahweh Ben Yahweh, I didn't question it," he said.

Still sporting a ponytail, Rozier was cheerful as he recalled riding the regional Metrorail transit line after dark with his sword in hand, looking for the right "white devils" to follow off the train and kill.

Initially, Rozier said, he was squeamish about Yahweh's requirement of bringing in a dead man's ear. But he learned that Yahweh meant what he said when the leader refused to credit his first two "white devil" murders because he hadn't brought in a trophy from the corpse.

He said he remedied that in September of 1986 when he and another defendant sliced off both ears of one murdered drifter. The act pleased Yahweh. "We got the day off and went to the movies," Rozier recalled.

Implicating other defendants in similar murders, Rozier recounted how one of them carried his proof in a jar. "The ear was floating in it," he said.

Rozier insisted that there was nothing personal about the killings as far as Yahweh Ben Yahweh was concerned.

"Any white devil would do," he said.

CHAPTER NINE

❧ ❧ ❧

King of the Israelites

HE LIKED TO refer to himself as a "Renaissance man," but he had the era wrong. He was more like a mad Medieval monk.

Nevertheless, by the end of the 1980s, Roch Theriault—middle-aged, balding, with pink-tinted eyeglasses and a bushy moustache that diverted attention from a weak chin and a perpetual, prissy scowl—was living what might have looked like the good life in a rustic utopia sixty miles northeast of Toronto. He was absolute ruler of a commune waiting for the end of the world—a man with eight wives, four male attendants, a golden crown, and even a royal title: King of the Israelites.

The world did not end, as Roch (pronounced "Rock") had predicted it would, in the cold Canadian woods. But after an eleven-year run, his self-contained world of glory did come crashing down in that most ignoble of personal apocalypses: with the police pounding on the door. In January of 1993 the sordid story of Roch Theriault and the Ant Hill Kids

—a cult centered on twisted homeopathic medicine, millenarian doom, and polygamy—began to unravel as Roch, forty-five years old, pleaded guilty to murder. He went to prison with followers still professing their belief in him, despite the fact that Roch had left two people dead and several others maimed for life, and bequeathed emotional duress to the twenty-five children that the Ant Hill leader and his eight wives brought into their wretched world.

It was the surgery that finally brought him down. Roch, whose medical knowledge came from an anatomy book, called it surgery, but the authorities had a more pointed term for it: butchery.

A prison psychiatrist would later evaluate him as "bright" and "sensitive," but neither description seemed to apply to Roch on September 28, 1988, the night the self-styled homeopathic healer and amateur anatomist operated on one of his wives.

Most cults have at least some connection with drugs, but the Ant Hill Kids were different. For Roch, battling cabin fever in the interminable Canadian winters, it was booze. And Roch was well-oiled already when thirty-two-year-old Solange Boilard—beautiful, trusting, looking for nothing more in life than certitude—complained that her stomach hurt.

Roch often took care of the medical needs of the commune with a complicated prescription of herbal remedies combined with prayer and New Age nostrums. But as time went on and the group's isolation and paranoia worsened in its run-down camp—and as the much-awaited end of the world failed to occur, as Roch had constantly predicted—more dramatic gestures were required. He completed the preparations wearing his ceremonial red velour robe and gold crown. Then he had Boilard strip naked and lie on a wooden table while the others gathered around.

Eerily calm, he prodded her abdomen, then suddenly punched her violently in the stomach and rolled her over. Pushing a plastic tube up her rectum, he forced a solution of hot molasses and vegetable oil into her.

She was told to turn on her back again for the next phase of the treatment. As she lay still, with her eyes closed, he raised a long hunting knife and slit her belly from the sternum to the navel. Ignoring her screams, he reached into the gaping wound in her abdominal cavity with bare hands and grabbed a section of her large intestine. He sliced it off and tossed it aside.

"There," he said. "That should do it."

Like surgeons he had seen in the movies, he held up his bloody hands. Ignoring the agonized screams coming from Boilard, Roch turned to Gabrielle Lavallée, who was standing by the table. "Close her up," he ordered.

Lavallee used a needle and thread to crudely stitch up the awful wound.

Astonishingly, Boilard lived through the night, shrieking in pain, before she finally died. The Ant Hill Gang buried her in the yard.

Roch Theriault was born in the tiny village of Riviere-du-Moulin, near Chicoutimi in Quebec Province, in 1947. The region is at the farthest point of deepwater navigation of the Saguenay River, one of the great water routes from the north and east down to the St. Lawrence. It is a rough-and-tumble commercial center, with a brisk tourist business and a prosperous trade in native handicrafts, especially wood-carving. This is where Roch first learned how to use a knife.

But he used it to make things at first. When he was about ten his parents moved with their seven children into a chilly cement bungalow in a small city of 20,000 called Thetford Mines, among the French-speaking population northeast of Montreal. The town's sole distinction is its unsightly expanse of open-pit mines, which supply 60 percent of the world's asbestos.

The boy was miserable. Back in Chicoutimi he had loved to wander the waterfront on errands with his father, who was a house painter. On these outings he would poke into the tiny galleries and shops clustered on wharves. The delicately carved artifacts, fashioned out of materials as ugly and crude as driftwood, had fascinated him. Life in Thetford Mines, in the industrial exurbs of Montreal, was grim and depressing.

"There was always somebody screaming or throwing something in that little house," a friend of one of his brothers said.

Roch's father liked to play an after-dinner game called "bone" with his three sons at the kitchen table. The rules of the game were that each person, in their heavy leather boots, would in turn kick the shins of the one sitting next to him, and the game would continue, with the pain escalating until someone cried *"Assez!"* Enough!

The game often went on for an hour or more. Roch was always the one to shout *"Assez!"*

In his abject unhappiness as a teenager, some of

Roch's future attitudes took root in the political and religious extremism of his father, who was a member of a secret right-wing Catholic organization called the "White Berets." Group members dressed in ceremonial costumes and engaged in rituals centered on their aim to combat liberal tendencies in the church.

Even in hard-bitten Thetford Mines, the Theriaults were considered low-class and odd, and the boy frequently wandered for long periods of time in the fields and woods, where he imagined he was communing with nature.

Later he would describe how he used these periods of solitude to learn about herbs and roots that could be used to cure disease. He cultivated an odd fantasy that he had hiked far into the wilderness and encountered a female bear tending to her cubs. The bear welcomed him into her lair and treated him like a cub until he wandered off again, Roch insisted.

Amazingly, people listened to him, perhaps because he was an entertaining talker in a place where lots of talk—and copious drinking—were the social nexus of life. "The girls especially liked him," a former friend said. "I think because he was so different from everyone else. He wasn't boring, you know?"

Even as a teenager, his friends turned to him for advice, especially about medical ailments. At a time in life when ailments are fairly simple—a cold, a toothache, a hangover, menstrual pain—this posed little problem for anyone, least of all Roch, who craved the attention. In time, he claimed to have begun experimenting on animals, and said he had learned to castrate cattle and pigs without any loss of blood.

In 1967, at the age of twenty, Roch married a

pretty local girl named Francine Grenier. They soon
had two children, and lived in a wood bungalow
down the road from his parents' house, where Roch
set up a small studio and shop to make and sell
handcrafted things—wood beer mugs, hand-carved
clocks, and souvenirs—to the trickle of hardy tourists
who had came through town in the warm months to
take guided tours of the asbestos pit mines or stop at
the local museum devoted to fossils and mining
equipment. He always had a knife in his hands, and
for a time it seemed to be providing him and his
family with a modest living. And it seemed like a
happy marriage—for a time.

But then Roch began making requests that his
young wife found strange. He insisted that she begin
wearing a long dark gown with a bonnet, "like a pio-
neer woman," he said. Then, unaccountably, he
would suddenly change his mind and order her to
wear a tiny miniskirt in public.

Meanwhile, he went to see her stern Catholic parents, who had a farm nearby, and asked them if they
would allow him to operate a campground for tourists on a section of their farm.

It would be a different kind of campground, he
told them. It would be for nudists. This is quite acceptable now, he explained.

His inlaws declined the offer to turn their acreage
into a nudist camp, and went to see their daughter.
Not long afterward, she left her husband, took the
two children, and moved back in with her parents on
the farm.

The single life allowed Roch to pursue his anatomy studies virtually full-time. He became obsessive
about it, and friends who knew him learned to avoid

chance conversations with Roch, who would capture any hapless audience and lecture for hours on the wonders of the human body.

At the same time, he joined a Catholic social organization to further enjoy his newfound bachelorhood. The group supported a local charity by holding regular dances, card parties, and other affairs. But soon after he became a member and was asked to head the initiation committee, Roch began lobbying to change the nature of the organization.

"He wanted us to wear these robes with religious symbols on them," said another former friend. "And he wanted us to elect him the leader."

Instead, he was stripped of his position.

Roch was a man who did not take rebuffs lightly. Furious, he quit not only the club, but the entire Roman Catholic church over the insult, and applied instead at the local Seventh Day Adventist church, where he quickly became obsessed with the sect's belief that the end of the world was imminent.

To prepare for the event, Roch began dressing in a hooded, ankle-length monk's robe. He said he was a prophet, and as such, he insisted that he be put in charge of the small but well-established local Seventh Day Adventist congregation.

He soon left them as well.

Again, Roch wandered in the wilderness. But this time he resurfaced not with a tale of a bear's kindness, but with a new role in life. He settled into a town north of Quebec, where he opened a shop that specialized in herbs, roots, and other supplies for the practice of homeopathic medicine. And he hung out a shingle as a healer.

"Roch was really a smart businessman," a person who knew him in this guise would later recall. "This was in the seventies, right around the time of all this 'whole-earth' interest in organic food and natural cures, and there he was. The place became like a local community center for the organic food nuts." His shop and clinic, in a clapboard building on the main street in town, became a center of New Age culture. And besides selling herbs and books, while dispensing medical advice, Roch also ran health seminars—including sessions on stopping smoking and losing weight. From these, he drew a following of young women who considered him something of a guru.

One of the most enthusiastic of these acolytes was twenty-six-year-old Giselle Lafrance, whom Roch married in 1977. Also frequent visitors at the clinic were a young married couple, Jacques and Maryse Giguere, who lived in town with their infant daughter. The Gigueres were so completely won over by Roch's "natural" approach to life and health medicine that Jacques even quit his construction job and Maryse quit her job at a local bakery; they sold their possessions and moved into Roch's house.

In time, Roch's clinic and residence began to resemble a commune. With Roch as the head of the business and the household, communal lifestyle began to resemble a family. Then, in late 1978, with winter setting in and the household strained under the crowded conditions, everything changed when Roch had his Great Vision.

It had come to him directly from God, he said to the assembled commune: the world was soon going to end in "a shower of boulderlike hailstones." Only a few of the chosen would survive. And the only way to do that was to flee society and live in the wilderness.

In his wanderings, Roch had already found his spot, if not in wilderness, at least in great desolation. It was on the north shore of the Gaspé Peninsula, at the mouth of the Gulf of St. Lawrence. Piled into two old cars and a pickup pulling a U-Haul with all of their possessions, the group—which now was comprised of Roch, four men, nine women, and four children—relocated to the Gaspé. They moved into three rented log cabins in a rugged valley where caribou and moose freely roamed. There, against the spectacular backdrop of the Chic-Choc Mountains, Roch presided over his commune with a new name. He called himself Moses. Each of the followers also took a name from the Bible.

As winter locked the commune in together, Moses said that the path to redemption would be arduous and full of pain.

He was not exaggerating.

During the first year of utopian isolation, cabin fever set in with a cold fury. Prayer, intimidation, and exhaustion held the group together. Scratching out a living was an exhausting drudgery of thirteen-hour days not far removed from the toils of the pioneers. For direction, the group was entirely dependent on Roch, who did little work himself. Instead, he drank starting in the late afternoon, and raged through dinner and long into the night, when anyone who crossed his path—man, woman, or child—was likely to feel the force of his boot or his hand.

The children especially were vulnerable. "He said

the children were disobedient and the devil had to be beaten out of them," Jacques Giguere recalled. "He justified beating our kids because he said we were too spiritually weak to do it ourselves."

The drunken, surly despot managed to keep his followers intimidated and dependent. After his drunken rages, he would collapse into bed and sleep until mid-afternoon, when he would get up to start the cycle all over again. Like most people close to a severe drunk, his followers were constantly off balance, not least because they themselves were drinking heavily. Sometimes Roch would spend his sober hours in nearly hysterical tears of shame and contrition, begging forgiveness, beseeching God to hear his pathetic pleas.

"Please God, do not ask me to beat the children any more!" he would wail, eyes heavenward.

But the prayers went unheeded. And the violence began anew, the women frightened into total submission, the men emasculated, the children anxious just to find a place to hide.

As theological glue to hold together this dysfunctional assemblage, Roch had cobbled a religious philosophy based on the tenets of Seventh Day Adventism, proclaiming over and over that "Jesus Christ will return in a premillennial, physical, imminent second advent. It will be visible, audible, and personal." While waiting for the great event, he was also enamored of certain historical aspects of another religion that is centered on the imminent end of the world—Mormonism. Polygamy especially attracted him, since he had already claimed for his own exclusive sexual use most of the women in the commune and convinced one man that, as a monk, he needed to remain celibate.

On several occasions during the first few years on the commune, Roch traveled to the U.S. to visit a well-known Mormon polygamist named Alex Joseph, who headed his own commune with at least nine wives and dozens of children in southern Utah, not far from the Grand Canyon. The fifty-five-year-old Joseph, himself a powerful figure who might have stepped from the Old Testament, liked the garrulous and intense Canadian well enough to invite him back at least twice during the 1980s. On their last meeting, the Utah patriarch held a solemn ceremony to present Roch with a gold-colored crown and conferred upon him a new title, King of the Israelites.

Imperially, Roch hurried back north and began acting the part in full glory. In the past, he had kept his relations with each of the women separate, but now he bedded them two and three at a time, and sometimes presided over contests to see which could claim the most orgasms.

He also staged games like a Roman emperor. That is, he ordered followers—men and women—to strip naked and compete in "gladiator" contests, fighting each other in a marked-off area while he casually held a stopwatch and awarded points for punches and knockdowns. Winners had to defend their victories from the next contender until the final contestant cried *"Assez!"* The contests went on for hours.

Roch and his wives were prolific all the while. Maternal instincts were still at work in 1981, when several of the women finally convinced Roch to allow the children to remain in a separate cabin while the adults gathered for their nightly prayer meetings, which always ended with one of Roch's tantrums.

Guy Veer, a twenty-three-year-old who had wandered into the commune after walking out of a hospital near Quebec, was designated to act as babysitter in the adjoining cabin. He was performing that duty one night when a two-year-old baby—the son of Jacques and Maryse Giguere—was severely beaten.

When the other adults discovered the battered child, they beseeched Roch to do something to help.

Gathering everyone around, he put the baby on the wooden table. Then he took a hunting knife and sliced into the boy's testicles to "relieve the pressure."

The child died screaming.

Roch accused the babysitter, Veer, and demanded that he be tried for murder. In a hastily convened "trial" presided over by Roch, the followers listened to testimony, weighed the evidence—and found Veer not guilty "by reason of insanity."

Unsatisfied with the verdict, Roch insisted that something had to be done to prevent Veer from ever fathering children himself. He ordered Veer held down on the table, where Roch sliced off the young man's testicles in a crude operation.

The next day, after Veer managed to stumble into town to get emergency medical assistance, the local clinic notified the police about the shocking case of mutilation on their hands.

For the first time, the authorities began interfering with Roch Theriault's twisted lifestyle. Though Roch tried to stonewall the police investigation, he and six of his followers were convicted of criminal negligence in the death of the baby, while Roch was also convicted in the castration of Veer.

He did not spend much time in jail. Released in 1984 after serving eighteen months, Roch set about reassembling his followers and attracting new ones in the organic-food circles.

Late in 1984, to circumvent a Quebec parole order barring Roch and his followers from associating again, the rejuvenated group moved to Ontario province, to a remote 200-acre tract of land that Roch had bought for $12,000 near Burnt River, about sixty miles northeast of Toronto.

Here they went to work again, like "busy ants," said one of the members, establishing a new utopia to await Armageddon under the direction of their master. This new community was financed by welfare checks, supplemented by a small crafts business opened in town. There, they sold wood carvings, knitted caps, handicrafts, and baked goods to locals and tourists. They called their business the Ant Hill Kids, a name that came to be applied to the commune as well.

At home, the sexually indefatigable Roch again kept the women barefoot and pregnant. Reestablished in his place, Roch was no longer content to be merely Moses and King of the Israelites. Now he was Abraham. As such, "he had to have many wives and children to keep the tribe going," said Gabrielle Lavallée, who had become his favorite wife.

However, the cult, having inserted itself into commercial society, drew the attention of local child-welfare authorities, who were interested in the large number of children living in a commune. Social workers with the Kawartha-Haliburton Children's Aid Society begin monitoring the commune closely, and stepped up their vigilance in 1985, after one of the babies at the Ant Hill Kids commune died of what the coroner ruled had apparently been natural causes.

By the end of the year they had accrued enough evidence of child abuse and neglect to move. In December, ten social workers and six police officers raided the commune, taking away fourteen children aged five months to sixteen years. The children—all fathered by Theriault—were placed with foster parents. In a very short time, authorities begin hearing stories some of the children were telling their new foster parents—that Theriault had forced them to take part in sexual acts.

Court records later quoted a six-year-old girl saying that he made the children masturbate him. Sometimes, she said, "Mom and me take turns."

Children's Aid workers questioned some of Roch's women. "They gave me two choices: 'Stay with Roch and lose your child, or leave Roch and keep him,'" Francine Laflamme, a cult member who was mother of one of the children taken away in 1985 and another in 1987 later told *Maclean's* magazine. "I decided I wasn't going to leave him, so they took my child. It was a very difficult decision."

All the while, the Ant Hill commune was a beehive of procreation. Between 1986 and 1988, Theriault's wives give birth to nine more of his children, but the child welfare authorities were utterly vigilant. As each child was born, it was removed to foster care. Finally, the commune was devoid of children.

That's when the violence got worse.

Roch punished anyone who displeased him, for minor infractions such as "sassing." One man who had said the wrong thing had a rubber band wrapped around his testicles. When the testicles swelled up to the size of an orange, Roch insisted that they had become infected. He had the others hold down the man, and he used a knife to slice open his scrotum, from which he cut out one testicle. Roch then cauterized the wound with a red-hot iron from the fire.

For the rest of the spring and summer, the Ant Hill Kids were busy with unending work. In late September, as the first signs of winter coming began to crawl over the northern trees, Boilard complained of the stomachache that led to her death at Roch's hands.

A week after they buried her in the yard, Roch ordered the Ant Hill Kids to dig up Boilard's corpse, insisting that death was merely a state of unconsciousness and that she could be brought back to life. As the group stood around the newly unearthed grave, gagging from the stench, Roch bent down and sliced open the decomposed flesh of the corpse's chest. He snapped off a skeletal rib, which he placed in a leather case he had made and wore around his neck. The body was then reburied.

A few weeks later, after drinking heavily for several hours, Roch again ordered everyone outside into the frigid pasture to dig up the grave. This time, while the others stood shivering in the cold, Roch—his red robes billowing in the icy wind—chanted prayers to bring Boilard back to life.

Crouching above the moldering remains, he ordered one of the men to go to a shed and bring back a hand saw. As he waited, he pulled the skull from the body.

Blowing on his hands to warm them, he used the saw to cut off the top section of the skull.

Then he ordered one of the women to masturbate him into the decomposed brain inside the skull.

Afterward, the remains were cremated.

Life at the commune went on for nearly one more year before the grisly incident that brought the police back.

In July of 1989, Gabrielle Lavallée, who had already lost eight teeth to Roch in an "operation" to treat a toothache, made the mistake of complaining about stiffness in one of her fingers, which adversely affected her work in the fields.

Gathering the others around, Roch had her place her hand on a wooden table. He then plunged a hunting knife into Gabrielle Lavalle's right hand, impaling it.

She stood there with her hand pinned to the table for almost an hour, afraid of losing consciousness "because if I did I knew he would kill me." Her arm turned black and blue during the ordeal. Roch said he knew how to treat that too.

He had her held, and then took a meat clever and hacked off her arm between the shoulder and elbow.

"On the first try, he didn't do the job because the blade was so dull," Lavellée later recalled. "The second time, the job was done."

She spent the night in agony, after which a fellow Ant Hiller crudely stitched the wound up. Several days later, when it had not stopped oozing blood, Roch used a blowtorch to heat up a piece of a drive shaft from a broken truck. As Lavellee shrieked, he cauterized the wound with the rod.

She managed to flee, using her good arm to flag down a motorist on a nearby road. She was taken to a hospital near Toronto, where the police questioned her about the injury.

When police arrived to raid the commune, everyone had fled. For six weeks police and Mounties searched the rugged terrain using helicopters and dogs. Finally, they captured Roch hiding with two of the women in a wilderness camp where he said he planned to spend the winter.

He spent the winter in court instead.

In October of 1989, Roch pleaded guilty for the assault on Lavallée. He was sentenced to twelve years in prison.

But then one of Roch's followers in custody told police about the death of Boillard. The police went to the site of the Ant Hill Kids commune and found her cremated remains.

Finally, in January of 1993, Roch pleaded guilty to the murder of Boilard, doing so with the expectation of leniency.

Before sentencing, Roch addressed the court with a long statement that expressed regret, but seemed to cast himself as the ultimate victim. Speaking in French, he said that being in prison had thus far afforded him the opportunity to do an "about-face" while enjoying "good vibrations" in assessing what he referred to as the "storm of unusual behavior in my inner self."

"Over several years, I made of myself an odious character, an incontestable master compelled undetectably by my own will and the oddities and debaucheries of my way of thinking, into which I had surreptitiously mixed love, hate, religion, labor, alcohol, and violence in my body's helpless state. I nourished my soul with the follies of grandeur.

"I have inflicted on myself mental wounds whose invisible scars I will carry for the rest of my life. Some of these scars will remain particularly vivid, such as the ones created when I carried out the folly of my fury, traumatizing, mutilating, and inflicting suffering on the members of my entourage, and most particularly the events that led to the premature death of Solange Boilard. I made a criminal of myself."

He acknowledged being the "leader of that commune" and accepted responsibility for what he called his "misdeeds."

And he concluded, "With dignity and a new integrity, I will serve whatever sentence the court deems suitable."

The sentence deemed suitable by the court was life in prison for the murder of Solange Boilard. Roch was transferred to a maximum security prison, Millhaven Institution, where he qualified to have regular conjugal visits in a trailer on the prison grounds from Francine Laflamme, the mother of his children. Two other of his "wives" moved in with Laflamme and opened a bakery, less than a mile from the prison gates.

Laflamme, meanwhile, maintained that she remained "madly in love" with Roch, whose "misdeeds" she blamed on alcohol and a diffcult childhood. "People try to make Roch sound like a monster, like a butcher," she told *Maclean's* magazine in 1993. "But he is not that. Most of the time he was not drinking and performing his operations. He was a marvelous man who was full of passion, intelligence, and originality. He loved to laugh and dance."

Roch also used his charm to win over some of his jailers, who judged him to be a model prisoner. A prison psychiatrist described him as "bright, inquisitive, and sensitive." Another prison evaluation described him as being "amenable to the rehabilitation process." He was even offered a transfer to a lesser security institution, but Roch turned it down when he found it would not include privileges of conjugal visits.

Under Canadian law, Roch Theriault, King of the Israelites, will be eligible for parole in the year 2000 —the year of the millennium.

CHAPTER TEN

☙ ☙ ☙

Ranch Apocalypse

BEFORE HE WENT down in flames and fury, Vernon Wayne Howell was living the good life, for a thirty-three-year-old prophet.

He was the absolute dictator of his own small world, which consisted of more than a hundred subjects living on seventy-seven acres of Texas brushland with, it turned out, enough guns to defeat a heavily armed force of federal agents.

As prophet, the gangly young man with unruly hair and soda-bottle-thick eyeglasses had the luxury of ranting and raving at his followers all night, and then sleeping all day while they went to work to pay the bills. There was money for travel, for vacations and recruiting in Australia, for pilgrimages to the Holy Land, for trips to Los Angeles to hook into fantasies of being a working musician. There was money to outfit a music room with expensive recording equipment to indulge Vernon's delusion that he was an accomplished heavy-metal guitarist who had merely chosen a more important line of work.

His command covered every aspect of life at the commune on the stubby prairie of central Texas, a half hour out of Waco. Vernon decided what food they ate—at one point decreeing a steady diet of nothing but bananas—what they thought, and who they slept with (Vernon himself had the right to select any woman to be his bed partner at any time).

"The angel of Revelation is what I claim to be," Vernon once said when asked who he thought he was.

The angel of Revelation heralds the end of the world. And for his gullible cult of followers, Vernon Howell in fact did just that.

Vernon was the illegitimate son of a mother who had given birth to him when she was fourteen. As a boy growing up near Dallas, he was a slow learner in school, where he claimed the other boys picked on him for his religious beliefs. When other boys were out playing, Vernon studied the Bible. According to his mother, Bonnie, he "memorized much of the New Testament before his thirteenth birthday." As a teenager, Vernon compensated for his awkwardness by body-building and playing the guitar, though he had no discipline for music lessons and preferred to rip along noisily with heavy-metal records drowning out his ineptness.

By the time he was twenty-one, Vernon had already been thrown out of his Seventh Day Adventist congregation for disrupting services by "ranting and raving." Imagining that he was being persecuted for his beliefs rather than for being an annoyance, Vernon drifted through Texas working menial jobs. In the early eighties he happened to come upon a small compound of people who were looking for a new prophet just about the same time that he was looking for an easier way to make a living.

He found it within this strange sect of religious fanatics who called themselves the Branch Davidians. When he found them, they were still encamped on a farm near Waco, as they had been for generations, waiting patiently for the end of the world.

The Davidians were a radical breakaway sect of the Seventh Day Adventists, a religious movement that began in the late 1830s amid the great fundamentalist and largely anti-Catholic religious "reawakening" that swept rural America. The founder was an evangelist named William Miller, who gathered a zealous group of followers who called themselves Adventists and were certain that the Second Coming was approaching. Miller even fixed the date: October 22, 1844. When the great day finally arrived without a sign of the triumphant Jesus on the horizon, the Adventists, in the indomitable logic of the true believer, decided that God had postponed the event because of the prideful expectation of the chosen, as well as the unworthiness of a sinful world. More diligent preparations were required. A disciple of Miller's, Ellen White, led the resurgent movement, now known as the Seventh Day Adventists, into the twentieth century.

The offshoot of Adventism that would be tapped by Vernon Howell was founded in 1930 by a Bulgarian immigrant, defrocked Adventist preacher and part-time washing machine salesman named Victor T. Houteff, who drifted from California with some followers and bought 189 acres of cheap farmland near Waco. There, he recruited new members for his commune through a Bible school, while refining a complicated theology based on scriptural "codes" that would unlock prophesies. While the leader was the only one who fully understood the complexities of the codes, all of the followers fervently believed the gist of the message, which was that Armageddon was about to arrive and that they themselves were the Elect who would rule the earth with Jesus Christ. Houteff believed that he had been personally chosen by God to cleanse the world of wickedness in preparation for the great event.

By the time Houteff died, with his sword still sheathed, in the mid-1950s, the commune had become something of a local joke: the Davidians' regular announcements that the end was coming, with the inevitable disappointments, were treated with gentle amusement in the local press. Still, the commune had the look of a permanent settlement. Besides the rambling wood-frame main building, with its meeting rooms, dining hall, and apartment for the prophet, there were a group of outbuildings, including dorm-like barracks to house followers and their families, though their number had declined to about forty at the time of Houteff's death.

Membership began picking up again when a paranoid evangelist named Ben Roden proclaimed himself prophet of the Davidians. He instituted mandatory daily worship services, and wisely resisted setting an actual date for the Second Coming. Roden was an avid pamphleteer who, among other things, blamed Watergate on the Pope. He also traveled frequently to Israel. When Roden died in 1978, he was succeeded by his wife, Lois, an energetic woman whose engaging personality and adeptness for publicity made her a well-known figure in the burgeoning world of fundamentalist evangelists branching out from the Southwest during the 1980s. Lois also liked to travel, and was especially fond of Australia, where she recruited new members.

She was prophet in 1981, the year that Vernon Howell, twenty-three years old, a ninth-grade dropout, itinerant con man, and frustrated guitarist with an exhaustive memory for Scripture—a fast-talking egotist with a love of the spotlight—wandered into the compound and asked to be accepted.

A humble supplicant, he introduced himself to Lois, now sixty-eight years old and beginning to lose her grip on the loyalty of the Davidians. Along with his quest for spiritual fulfillment, Vernon told Lois and her followers, he sought help to overcome what he said was his major vice, excessive masturbation.

Sensing that her group needed new blood, Lois welcomed the intense young man into the fold. Though many of the older followers regarded him as the camp bum and shiftless would-be hippie, Vernon quickly made himself useful doing clean-up work in the kitchen, making small repairs to the run-down communal buildings, even fixing broken-down cars that members used for routine errands to and from town, where many worked day jobs. His quick smile and religious zeal soon won him many friends—including Lois herself. By the end of 1983, after persuading the old woman that he had a vision in which God had shown him that they must conceive a son together, a son who would become the last prophet, Vernon and Lois were having a sexual relationship.

This relationship became known at a time when

some Davidians were already muttering misgivings about Lois, who had taken to reciting the Lord's Prayer with a new twist: "Our Mother, which art in heaven."

From his position as Lois's lover, Vernon craftily began to exploit the power vacuum he perceived within the Davidians, who he maintained had become spiritually flabby and undisciplined—and more than ready for rigorous rejuvenation under a younger leader ordained by God. Calling on his natural if undeveloped abilities as an entertainer, Vernon emerged as a Bible-thumping camp revivalist, thrilling long-bored Davidians to the souls of their beliefs with hellfire-and-brimstone sermons that the Apocalypse at last was near and preparations for the great battle must begin. Under his urgent preaching, the commune united in an atmosphere of impending crisis.

Sensing his growing power, Vernon became emboldened enough to leave Lois for a wife at the other end of the age scale—a fourteen-year-old girl, Rachel Jones, whose parents were members of the group. She bore Vernon's first two children, a son, Cyrus, and a daughter, Star. Venturing to describe himself to wide-eyed Davidians as "the ultimate sex machine," Vernon also induced other young females into his bed, among them one girl aged ten.

All the while, the upstart's growing influence was monitored resentfully by Lois's heir-apparent, her forty-five-year-old son, George, a surly and rotund man with a great bushy beard, who wore a ten-gallon hat on his head and a pistol on his belt. Behind his back some of the more worldly Davidians had taken to referring to George derisively as the "Prince of

Whales." It was a cruel allusion both to his ungainly size and to the fact that he had reached middle-age, like the heir to the British crown, still waiting for his mother to die so he could assume the throne.

When Lois did die suddenly in 1984, George moved decisively against his rival, whom he had denounced in a newsletter as a "rock and roller musician and a Satan worshiper," an "adulterer," and a "bastard" who was "prohibited from the congregation unto the tenth generation."

Vernon was not yet prepared to fight. He announced he was leaving the commune. To George's astonishment, twenty-five followers, including many of the younger members of the group, left with him.

This began a year-long period of wandering for Vernon and his devout band of believers. Now regarding themselves as the chosen people in exile, they traveled in a couple of beat-up vans like a band of Gypsies, picking up odd jobs and Social Security checks for support, recruiting new followers throughout the Southwest, even managing to gather enough money to send Vernon on trips to Israel—where he became convinced that he was the prophet who would lead the righteous to battle with Satan. Like his predecessors the Rodens, he also visited Australia, and brought new believers back with him.

Meanwhile, in New Orleans proselytizing on the fringes of a national convention of Seventh Day Adventists, Vernon concluded that the classic rock anthem by the Animals, "House of the Rising Sun," somehow contained the code that would unlock his prophesy that the end of time was rapidly approaching.

Working uncharacteristically hard, he even managed to learn to play the song on the guitar, in the company of a handful of other failed rock musicians who had wandered into the group, which now numbered more than sixty people, including young couples with children.

Vernon's splinter group eventually settled back in Texas, on a small commune in a town called Palestine. In 1987, Vernon and his Praetorian guard of body-builders and bullies who called themselves the Mighty Men came up with a plan to sneak down to Waco and storm the Mount Carmel compound, to wrest it from the control of George Roden.

Alarmed by Vernon's reappearance on the scene, George had challenged the upstart to the ultimate faith-healing test: On Halloween night of 1987, the corpse of an eighty-five-year-old Davidian buried on the property was dug up. Only if Vernon could raise it from the dead, George declared, would he be able to call himself prophet.

Vernon had a better idea. Declaring George the "anti-Christ," Vernon led seven armed cohorts in military camouflage uniforms onto the Mount Carmel compound in a predawn raid a few days afterward. In the skirmish, George was shot and wounded.

Vernon and his men were charged with attempted murder. While on bail, they moved back into the Mount Carmel compound and began fortifying it. George wisely fled. After a highly publicized trial during which Vernon and his cohorts held court regularly with reporters, a jury failed to reach a verdict on Vernon and returned a verdict of acquittal on the others. The triumphant Vernon—rejoicing in the publicity—invited the public to the compound for an ice cream social.

New recruits came in, not only from Texas but from the network that Vernon had established on his travels at home and abroad. The resurgent Davidians now had about 125 members, and Vernon declared himself their prophet with an edict that left little uncertainty about the extent of his authority. "It means that the prophet owns everything—your house, your money, even your underwear," he explained. "That means when the prophet comes to your house at night and asks you to strip naked, you are obligated by God to hand over your underpants."

With such sweeping powers, Vernon decided he needed a new name. He legally changed his to David (after King David) Koresh (the Hebrew name for Cyrus, the Babylonian king who allowed the Jews back into the Israel), and announced that he was the seventh and final prophet, the man who would prepare the Davidians to stand up to Satan. Armageddon would begin—soon—with a U.S. Army attack on the Davidian compound, Vernon declared. Mount Carmel itself was renamed. It became Ranch Apocalypse.

Meanwhile, it was imperative that the prophet himself be prolific. Compliant followers allowed Vernon to choose his "wives" at will from among their own spouses and daughters; the wives' status was indicated by Star of David pendants they wore.

At the same time, compound life became markedly militaristic, with armed guards posted at the perimeters and regular defensive drills scheduled to prepare for the imminent battle. Carefully, Koresh introduced paranoia into the general sense of crisis, deftly tightening the group's psychological isolation. The effect was calculated: Every day, the outside world was made to seem an ever more hostile place, brimming with enemies and treachery. Within the compound, the prophet provided security and solace, and all the answers. Every form of activity, from sexual relationships to the games children were allowed to play, was subject to Koresh's direct supervision. Nightly, Davidians assembled to watch video war movies chosen by Koresh. Afterward, they sat through the prophet's harangues, sometimes in all-night sessions. Any whisper of dissension was promptly reported to the prophet, and dealt with severely.

By 1989, with Koresh claiming the right to have sex with anyone he chose at any time he chose, families were effectively destroyed as functioning social units. Men and women were segregated in separate dorms, and children were housed apart from their parents. To compensate the men for the loss of their self-esteem, Vernon even thought of a safety valve, encouraging them to drink heavily.

"We as Davidians aren't interested in sex," one of the men whose wives had been claimed by Koresh would later explain to reporters. "Sex is so assaultive, so aggressive. David has shouldered that burden for us."

In such an atmosphere, each outlandish assertion built the foundation for the next one. According to another Davidian, Koresh told devotees that "if they remained faithful, God would one day return and take them to heaven in his spaceship." Increasingly, Koresh's harangues centered around the idea that many of the followers would have to die, violently, before that could come about.

While followers stayed awake through the all-night ravings that sometimes didn't end until it was time to stagger off to work in the morning, Koresh and his Mighty Men maintained an active social life outside the compound, regularly visiting local rock and country-western bars to hang out with musicians, or poking around regional gun shows looking for weapons to buy or trade. They amassed an arsenal at Ranch Apocalypse.

Outwardly, the usual sense of dotty serenity appeared to prevail at the compound. Davidians had always been known as good neighbors, quietly pleasant if somewhat eccentric, God-fearing, always available to jump-start a stalled car or help out a neighbor in need. There were rumors, however. Little girls being used for sex. Beatings. And, of course, the guns and other weapons piling up. A UPS man delivering a package that ripped open was surprised to find a box of hand grenades inside. It was said the Davidians had enough armaments on hand to supply a small army—which of course was exactly what Koresh had in mind.

For four years, one follower, Mark Breault, an amateur musician who had once believed fervently in Koresh, watched the world turn upside down at Ranch Apocalypse. Breault was, in fact, one of the original Mighty Men. But in 1989, after his wife had already left the compound to return to Australia, he decided it was time to rejoin her. At dawn one day, Breault was listlessly playing a Star Trek video game in an office near Koresh's quarters in the main building when he encountered a thirteen-year-old girl who had just spent the night with the prophet.

"Good morning," he told the child.

"What are you doing here?" she demanded imperiously. Breault, who had been keeping a detailed diary of his time at Ranch Apocalypse, thought the girl was acting "like the Queen of England."

"I'm just doing some work," he told her. Defensively, he deleted the video game from the computer screen and called up a business document, to show that he was working. The girl came over to examine the screen briefly, nodded, and walked away.

Feeling a mixture of relief and disgust, Breault decided it was time to go. He had seen Vernon repeatedly break nine of the Ten Commandments. He didn't plan on being around to see the last one go down: Thou shalt not kill.

To get the money to flee without stirring Koresh's suspicions, Braeult slipped away from the compound to call his wife in Australia, where a small group of former Davidians were openly expressing their fears about what they had seen going on at the Waco complex before they themselves had left. She agreed to send him the money for air fare from Los Angeles to Melbourne. To get to Los Angeles, he told Koresh that his keyboard mixer was on its last legs and he needed to drive there to buy a new one. Koresh said he would go along. They would stay for nearly a month at a house in Pomona owned by Davidians. The thirteen-year-old girl made the drive with them. Koresh brought along an AK-47 hidden in the trunk.

Breault almost didn't escape. At the California house, Koresh confronted him, saying he had heard reports from California associates about Breault's bad "attitude." Breault was ordered to pack his bags and fly back to Waco to await his punishment.

Breault packed his bags but went in the opposite direction, getting on the plane to Australia. It was a decision that saved his life.

In Australia, Breault began organizing the former followers—people still living in terror of death threats from Koresh and associates back in America. Finally, they decided to sound the alarm, hiring a private detective to further their case and spread the warning that Koresh, a madman exercising maniacal control over a group of largely innocent people, was planning to go down in flames to fulfill his prophesies, and kill them all in the process.

Under constant threats from Texas, but fortified by Breault's detailed diaries, tape recordings of Koresh's rantings, and their own memories, the frightened Australian rebels went to work documenting evidence that they hoped would get the attention of U.S. law enforcement authorities. Segments on the group's warnings were aired by the Australian edition of *A Current Affair*. One former member recounted that Koresh "always said the authorities would never take the children away from him. He'd rather kill them before giving them up."

"The only time the authorities are going to do something is when there's a pile of bodies," a sympathizer at the Waco compound wrote secretly to the breakaways in Australia. "It'll be another Jonestown . . ."

For two long years, as Koresh armed his camp and

prepared for Armageddon, their warnings went largely unheeded.

In 1992, however, the U.S. Bureau of Alcohol, Tobacco, and Firearms—ATF—did begin an investigation into the widespread reports of weapons at the Waco compound. ATF undercover agents dispatched to the scene tried to inflitrate the group. Their efforts were a joke to Koresh, who openly ridiculed the undercover agents—middle-aged men trying to pass themselves off as college students trying to befriend Davidians. By now Koresh and his lieutenants had stockpiled eleven tons of arms—including three hundred firearms and battlefield armaments such as .50 caliber antitank rifles.

"We will put a weapon in everyone's hand," Koresh had told his followers. "If you want to die for God, you must be willing to kill for God."

At other times, he warned Davidians that their own deaths would not be enough—they would also have to kill outsiders who would be coming for them. "You can't die for God if you can't kill for God," he warned.

By November of 1992 the ATF had enough evidence to obtain a search warrant and a warrant for Koresh's arrest on federal firearms charges. But executing it was not going to be easy. For months the ATF force, which had grown to a hundred agents, supplemented by local police and Texas Rangers, drilled for the raid on the compound. The operation was given the code name Operation Trojan Horse. From inside Ranch Apocalypse, Koresh watched with grim amusement.

"They are waiting to get zapped up to heaven,

where they'll be transformed to fight a war where they get to kill all their enemies," according to a newspaper account in early 1993, when the sect's growing size and the activities of the ATF had begun to attract more media attention.

They didn't have to wait long.

The ATF raid was set for Sunday, February 28, 1993. The day before, the Waco *Herald-Tribune* had begun publishing a series of articles on the cult, based on months of reporting about what the paper called "this menace in our community."

Though the ATF plan was predicated on secrecy, it was clear to anyone in the vicinity of the Davidian compound what was going on, as agents and cops donned battle gear, and assault and communications vehicles lumbered along rural roads. Agents were transported to the scene in two cattle trailers. Nearby, a public relations officer for the ATF was waiting with a stack of press releases announcing the successful arrest of Koresh.

As three National Guard helicopters clattered in over the plains, the raid began. Agent Roland Ballesteros, a six-year veteran of the ATF, was the first one to the front door, which was open. Koresh was standing just inside, apparently unarmed. Ballesteros saw that he was smiling. Then Koresh slammed the door.

At the wheel of one of the cattle trailers, ATF agent Dan Curtis was worried about the eerie quiet at Ranch Apocalypse, where people usually could be seen moving about.

"I think we're in trouble," he told the men with him.

Within seconds gunshots erupted from within the

compound. The raiding force was immediately pinned down under intense fire.

Though it had been planned on the premise of secrecy, the operation could have taken an ad out in the paper announcing its schedule, for all the stealth involved. All night long local roads had been crowded with emergency vehicles. By first light, reporters and neighbors in the vicinity were openly discussing the raid. A woman on the scene in a truck hired to supply agents with doughnuts and coffee even encountered Davidians discussing the imminent assault outside the compound.

Koresh was clearly aware. Nevertheless, the raid went on as scheduled in the belief that with a quick show of force, Koresh could be made to come to reason and give up.

Early Sunday morning, Koresh had been leading a Bible session when a follower rushed into the compound to say he had encountered a local television crew setting up to cover the raid.

"They're coming," the prophet announced, looking out the window across the frame buildings to the scrub brush where the assault force, wearing blue jumpsuits and flak jackets, was assembled. "The time has come."

Over the police radio, reporters monitoring the traffic heard a report from an unknown person. "There's no guns in the windows. Tell them it's a go."

In a great rush, agents rushed out of the cattle trailers and hoisted ladders to the roof of the main building. Suddenly, gunfire erupted from points all over the compound. Some of the agents went down.

As the battle raged, Koresh picked up the phone

and called the county sheriff's department, where Lieutenant Larry Lynch took the call.

"You killed some of my children!" the prophet screamed. "There's a bunch of us dead now, and a bunch of you guys dead now. That's your fault!"

"Who am I speaking with?" Lynch asked, trying to stay calm.

"The notorious," Koresh replied. "What did you guys do that for?"

"What I am doing is trying to establish some communications links with you."

"No, no, no, no, no!" said Koresh. "Let me tell you something. You see, you brought a bunch of guys out here and you killed some of my children. We told you we wanted to talk. We knew you were coming and everything. We knew even before you knew!"

Lynch tried to persuade Koresh to stop shooting, but it was useless. Knowing the call was being widely monitored, Koresh took the opportunity to deliver a sermon. "See, we will serve God first," he declared. "We will serve the god of the church . . ."

After listening to this for a minute, Lynch interrupted, "We can talk theology, but not now."

Koresh protested, "No! This is life and death!"

"That's what I'm talking about," Lynch said.

Retorted Koresh, "Theology is life and death!"

During the battle, Koresh claimed he had been shot in "the gut" and phoned his mother in Chandler, Texas, leaving a message on her answering machine: "Hello, Mama, it's your boy. They shot me and I'm dying, all right? But I'll be back real soon, okay? See y'all in the skies."

The battle lasted less than an hour. When the smoke cleared, four ATF agents and six Davidians were dead. Another twenty-four ATF agents were injured. In all, more than a quarter of the ATF force had been casualties. Inside Ranch Apocalypse, at least one of the dead Davidians had been wounded in the shooting and executed by comrades to "put him out of his misery."

The raid, broadcast on national television, was a debacle for the ATF, which found itself on the defensive against charges of lax security, poor planning, and gross incompetence. "We were outgunned," a spokesman for the ATF weakly explained. As reinforcements poured in, the FBI was put in charge of what would become a fifty-one-day siege at Ranch Apocalypse.

Inside the compound, Koresh was now a man looking into the pit of hell, but he seemed to have made a miraculous recovery from the gunshot wound he reported to his mother. In no time he was back on the phone, giving long and rambling interviews on radio and television stations. All the while, he harangued the FBI's elite squad of terrorist-hostage negotiators with ravings about the end of the world.

At first the FBI negotiators on the scene pursued a conciliatory approach, aware that Koresh's followers were desperate religious fanatics engaged in what criminologists call the "gamble with death." There were some initial signs of success in the approach, since at the end of the first week of the siege, Koresh allowed twenty-one children and two elderly women to leave the compound. That, authorities calculated, left forty-seven women, forty-three men, and seventeen children inside. It was known they had food stockpiled to last for over a year. It was not known at that point how many weapons they had, or how determined Koresh was to go down in flames and take everyone with him. All anyone had were guesses.

And soon they began guessing wrong. As the siege stretched on through the weeks, FBI negotiators cautioning patience began losing ground to more tactical-minded agents pressing for "tightening the noose" with a show of force, and employing psychological warfare techniques to show the Davidians who was in charge. A memo from two FBI agents on the negotiating team cautioned that such tactics, "if carried to excess, could eventually be counterproductive and could result in loss of life." But the warning was discounted by authorities determined to show the Davidians that they meant business.

Koresh harangued his followers by night and his tormentors by day. Hostage experts on the scene apparently were unprepared to deal with a madman who had convinced more than a hundred people that their deaths meant their salvation—it seemed the cops and the cultists barely spoke the same language. Once, when Koresh told negotiators that he was working to put into effect his final interpretation of the fabled seven seals that apocalyptic Scripture stated had to be opened before the end of the world, one of the agents believed that Koresh was making an environmental allusion about the plight of sea seals.

In Australia, Mark Breault and his associates watched with mounting horror. One of those "seals," as interpreted by Koresh, was mass suicide.

"I told the FBI that Koresh believed the fifth seal taught suicide and martyrdom," Breault said later. "Koresh further believed that God had ordained a fixed number of martyrs, and this number was almost complete. The end of the world could only take place when this was done . . . I emphasized over and over that a mass suicide posed the greatest danger. I said further that I did not believe Koresh would ever give up."

As the siege continued for months with no end in sight, FBI hostage negotiators were reaching the point of exhaustion. In Washington, federal authorities were baffled by conflicting reports and theories about the situation in Waco. Some echoed the dire warnings that Koresh's group was an insane cult, ready for mass suicide. Others insisted that Koresh was holding his followers hostage and would listen to reason if forced to, pointing to the fact that he had already let some people go. Meanwhile, agents on the scene stepped up the campaign of psychological warfare. They set up a bank of loudspeakers that blasted the Davidians for nights on end with rock music, chanting of Tibetan monks, even recorded screams of dying rabbits. Searchlights were pointed at windows of the compound's main building and dorms.

Inside Ranch Apocalypse, Davidians hauled bales of hay in to barricade walls and windows. Windows were covered with cloth. The electricity from the camp's generator failed. The flicker of camp lanterns glowed through the night in darkened windows.

In Washington in mid-April the FBI went to Attorney General Janet Reno, who had been on the job for less than a month, with a detailed plan to storm the compound and release the hostages in a lightning

strike that would begin with armored vehicles pump-
ing in tear gas. Reno, who already had been apprised
that children were being sexually abused by Koresh,
was also worried about the effect of deteriorating
sanitary conditions inside the compound. She was
assured that the tear gas to be used was nonlethal
and would not start what authorities feared most,
perhaps recalling the Move disaster in Philadelphia:
a fire. Furthermore, the FBI's vaunted psychological
profile team, which had been dispatched to the scene
to evaluate Koresh, had concluded that he was a personal coward who probably didn't have enough claim
on his followers' loyalty to enact a mass suicide like
the one in Jonestown. After assuring President Clin-
ton that gassing the compound and flushing them out
was "the best way to go," Reno warily gave the go-
ahead on April 17.

On the morning of April 19, fifty-one days after
ATF agents had been mowed down on the first assault in February, after weeks of tense negotiations
and broken promises from Koresh, the raiders
donned battle gear and moved into place starting at
4:30 A.M. There were 170 FBI agents on the scene.
They had fitted two M-60 tanks with booms to poke
holes into the walls of the compound's buildings. Armored personnel carriers lumbered into place behind them.

A brisk wind whipping over the plains caused con-
cern that the tear gas could dissipate too quickly.
Tensely, the agents waited for the wind to die.

Finally, a minute before six A.M., FBI hostage ne-
gotiator Byron Sage called the compound and spoke
with one of Koresh's top aides, Steve Schneider.

"There's going to be tear gas injected into the compound. This is not an assault. Do not fire. The idea is to get you out of the compound."

"You're going to gas us?" Schneider asked incredulously.

In response, the phone was ripped away from the wall and thrown out the window.

"Everybody grab your gas masks!" agents heard someone shout from within as the loudspeakers blasted a warning to Davidians waking sleepy-eyed in their dorms:

"This is not an assault! Do not fire! Come out now and you will not be harmed!"

Inside, preparations quickened. Some of the children were fitted with gas masks. Koresh, wearing sweat pants and a tank top, put on a camouflage hunting vest with pockets for ammunition. Knots of Davidians quietly gathered to read Bibles and pray.

At six A.M. a tank lumbered up to the outside of the main building and halted while the loudspeaker continued to blare, "This is not an assault! Do not fire! Exit the compound and follow instructions!"

In response, a burst of gunfire came from inside the compound.

Under fire, the tank lurched forward, its ram knocking a hole in a corner of the building. Behind it, other armored vehicles advanced, leveling their rams to punch more holes in walls. Tear gas began hissing inside. By now, firing from within the compound was intense. The agents did not return fire.

The first phase of the gassing operation went on for a half hour. The plan, an FBI official said, was "gas and negotiate, gas and negotiate." When none of the Davidians surrendered, more gas was pumped in. By 8:30 A.M. the wind was picking up again. Davidians with rifles silently fell into place beside the haystack barricades at windows. Fleetingly, Koresh himself was seen at an exposed window, checking gas masks on followers before he ducked out of sight.

At 11:50 came another round of tear gas. Again the authorities waited. As they did, a high-tech listening device that had been placed ten feet from the front door of the compound picked up the following comments from unidentified voices: "I want a fire around the back. Let's keep that fire going." Within minutes FBI snipers on high ground overlooking the compound reported seeing two men setting small fires at either side of the complex.

Thin curls of smoke now rose from the front of the compound. At the same time, an FBI surveillance plane circling overhead reported that small fires had broken out behind the tower and at several other points inside Ranch Apocalypse. A few terrified Davidians ran out into the clear and were taken into custody. Bales of hay began burning at several locations inside the main building.

With the wind now blowing briskly, the ramshackle compound burst into huge flames. Explosions roared as ammunition stockpiles caught fire. The rickety watchtower over the main building collapsed in a fireball.

"What is the plan?" one man inside shrieked to Koresh.

"Well, you always wanted to be a charcoal briquet," the prophet replied.

Inside the compound Koresh unleashed a torrent

of bloody choreography as the Davidians' world came to an end.

When it was done, horrified authorities would find in the rubble the charred bodies of Koresh and seventy-five of his followers, twenty-five of them children under the age of fifteen. Twelve of those children had been fathered by Koresh. Autopsies would reveal that Koresh had died of a bullet wound in the forehead, apparently self-inflicted. The body of his chief lieutenant, Steve Schneider, had a gunshot wound in the mouth. Seventeen other Davidians, including five children, died of gunshot wounds before they were burned. One woman was shot in the back. A two-year-old boy had been stabbed to death. Eight members of the cult had managed to escape the holocaust, some of them fleeing with their clothes in flames.

Later, eleven Davidians—several of whom were not at the compound during the initial February 28 raid—were charged with murder and conspiracy in the deaths of the ATF agents. One Davidian, thirty-four-year-old Kathryn Schroeder, a former Air Force sergeant whose husband had been killed in the initial shootout and whose four children were among those released by Koresh in March, and who had herself fled the compound on March 12, pleaded guilty to a reduced charge of resisting arrest in exchange for testimony that the Davidians had a well-established shoot-to-kill battle plan to repel any raid on the compound.

At the trial in 1994, the prosecutor, assistant U.S. Attorney William Johnston, declared that Koresh and all those who stayed in the compound were willing participants in a "conspiracy" that led to the deaths of the federal agents.

Dick DeGueron, a Houston lawyer who had represented Koresh throughout the fifty-one-day standoff, told reporters, "They sincerely believed the world was going to end—and end in catastrophe."

In February 1994 the jury sent a clear admonishment to the government, rejecting the murder and conspiracy charges against all eleven defendants. Instead, five were convicted of voluntary manslaughter in the killing of the four ATF agents. They and two others were also convicted of various firearms violations. Four defendants were acquitted of all charges.

Clearly, authorities had learned little from the lessons of Jonestown and Philadelphia. They still had not come to understand and appreciate the ferocious determination of a cult that would kill, and die, in order to survive.

Koresh's movement did not completely vanish in the flames of Waco. Some survivors who had not been criminally charged remained faithful to Koresh in the months after the showdown. One, Mary Jones, one of the prophet's mothers-in-law, maintained her loyalty even though her husband was killed in the February shootout, and two of her daughters, a son, and four grandchildren all perished in the April 19 fire. "I just find great relief in the prophesies of the coming kingdom," she would insist afterward.

Failure and defeat simply does not exist in such a mind-set. "We see his departure as a sign from God," said Janet McBean, a Koresh follower who had been away from the compound when it was destroyed. She insisted that survivors were awaiting Koresh's resurrection from the dead. Then the

Davidians would themselves rise from their blackened ashes to battle the legions of Satan on earth.

"The next meeting point for all of us is in heaven," she said. "Then we'll come down and we'll set it up."

CHAPTER ELEVEN

Circle of Fire

"HERE EVERYTHING IS white. Outside is darkness," Luc Jouret would lecture his disciples, well-educated, affluent believers in New Age metaphysics who dressed in ceremonial robes and banqueted in secret chambers. "We are in a circle of fire. Everything is being consumed. We are about to make a leap in macroevolution," said Jouret, a handsome, soft-spoken environmental idealogue, a forty-six-year-old homeopathic physician with sparkling eyes, curly black hair, and a gentle face—a man who would never hurt a tree, but had no problem consigning fifty-three men, women, and children to their deaths in a holocaust of flames and gunfire.

Jouret's followers, members of a group called the Solar Temple, made that great leap on a cool night early in October of 1994 and went to their deaths in a blazing orgy of murder and suicide on two continents.

"Death can represent an essential stage of life," Jouret had said on one of the dozens of motivational audiotapes he and his followers marketed through New Age bookstores and outlets.

As always, authorities searching through the embers and trying to identify the bodies could only shake their heads in bafflement at what would cause a close-knit group of people to follow a man to their deaths for no apparent reason other than blind faith.

At least some members of the group left behind rambling suicide notes that began arriving in the offices of law enforcement authorities and news organizations days after the bodies were found at two locations in Switzerland and one in Canada. "We are leaving this earth to find in all lucidity and freedom a new dimension of truth and absolution, far from the hypocrisies and oppression of this world, in order to achieve the seeds of our future generation," said one. A document received by the *New York Times* was titled "Transit for the Future," and predicted that the earth would soon suffer destruction along with lines of the biblical Sodom and Gomorrah. Still other documents intimated that Luc Jouret and other leaders of the cult chose to "leave this earth prematurely" because they were being persecuted.

Of course, not all of the victims died willingly. As usual, there were those who resisted. One Solar Temple document sent to newspapers alluded to that fact, saying that some of those who went to their deaths that terrible night had to be "gently" killed, for their own eternal good.

One of Switzerland's leading cult specialists, Jean-Francois Mayer, told reporters he had received three such documents in the mail after the deaths. They were signed, "Mr. Depart."

* * *

Who were these people who called themselves "Knights of Christ" and thought they had the key to eternal life? Most of what they left behind was depressingly familiar: weapons stockpiled against an imagined assault; evidence of a fanatical, paranoid belief that the world was coming to an end and that they somehow were at the center of the great drama; denunciations of persecution. But as the millennium approaches and doomsday cults grow in number, the Solar Temple contributed something new to the evolution. These were no wild-eyed Bible-thumpers holed up on a remote farm, waiting to do battle with Satan. Rather, these were affluent people, for the most part well-educated and accomplished. They formed a thoroughly modern killer cult that deftly dipped into the zeitgeist of the 1980s—the Solar Temple evidently was plugged into international financial networks of the global economy—and cloaked it with 1990s elements of New Age mysticism and environmental activism.

They died on a night of horror.

The first alarm was raised on October 5, 1994, by a farmer named Fernand Thierrin, gazing out his window while he sipped a postmidnight nightcap of cognac in a pastoral Swiss farming village of Cheiry, about fifty miles northeast of Geneva.

Thierrin noticed a red glow on the hill about a mile from his house. Then he saw flames lick at the dark autumn sky. He called the village fire department and got into his car to drive toward the flames.

The first one to arrive at the blazing farmhouse, Thierrin smashed his way inside and found the owner, seventy-two-year-old Albert Giacobino, a retired businessman, dead in his bedroom. But even in the smoke and danger of a burning house, it was clear that fire hadn't killed the man. Giacobino had been shot to death.

As firemen arrived and brought the flames under control, a more thorough search was made of the main house and outbuildings. In the spacious barn, untouched by the flames, firefighters opened a door to find a chapel with red-satin walls and an occult pentagraph drawn on the red-carpeted floor. There were twenty-three bodies fanned in an sunburst circle around a triangular pulpit, under a painting of a Christlike figure, which in fact resembled Luc Jouret, holding a chalice and with a rose above its head. Ten of the dead were men, clad in ceremonial robes—some red, some black, and a few white, indicating a hierarchy of sorts. Twelve were women, all dressed in flowing gold and white gowns. And one was a twelve-year-old girl, later identified as the daughter of Joseph DiMambro, Jouret's chief lieutenant.

Half of the corpses had plastic bags tied around their faces. Several had died with their hands bound. And twenty of the bodies had bullet wounds in the head; some had been shot as many as eight times. Around the corpses were empty champagne bottles, which were also found in an adjoining chapel that had walls of mirrors.

Undamaged in the fire was a cassette recording, a rambling discourse on the earth and astrology, with allusions to mass suicide. The mystery deepened when police realized that three rifles had been found on the scene, but that the fifty-two bullet casings on the floor had come from a .22 caliber pistol that was not found. Where was the gun, and more important, where was the person who had fired it?

The answer to that aspect of the mystery, at least, came four hours later, as dawn streaked the jagged mountain peaks looming over the Alpine hamlet of Granges-sur-Salvan, fifty miles to the southeast of Cheiry. Suddenly, there was an explosion that rocked the village a mile away; flames leaped out at three adjoining ski chalets that had been used by Jouret and members of the Solar Temple.

When firefighters battled their way inside and subdued the flames, they found twenty-five bodies, mostly lying on beds. Five of them were children. No one here had been shot, but some of the bodies showed signs of severe beatings. In the smoldering ashes were supplies of tranquilizers, hypodermic syringes, and intravenous drips. The victims had been heavily drugged, and then burned to death. Residues of plastic trash bags were found melted on some of the heads, indicating they had died with the bags over their faces. On the floor was the .22 pistol that had been used hours before in Cheiry.

During ceremonies, members were said to have worn plastic bags on their heads to symbolize the defilement of the earth's environment. The *Village Voice* sardonically referred to that as "the Solar Temple's most imaginative rite: confessing your sins against nature with a plastic bag on your head."

But the carnage of October 5 was not confined to Switzerland.

In Canada, at a duplex ski chalet fifty miles northwest of Montreal that was among the extensive real estate holdings of Jouret and DiMambro, the news from Switzerland came with a direct connection to a horror scene police had just discovered there.

Early on the morning of October 5 a fireball had suddenly exploded and engulfed the Canadian chalet in flames. Firefighters responding to the blaze found the bodies of a man and a woman in a bedroom. Each wore medallions with a double-headed eagle and the initials for the Solar Temple.

But these were not the only victims. As investigators worked through the chalet, they found in the basement the bodies of two adult members of the sect, a thirty-five-year-old Swiss man, Antonio Dutoit, and his thirty-year-old British wife, Nicki Dutoit. Antonio had been DiMambro's chauffeur and handyman; Nicki had been a babysitter for DiMambro. A few hours later still another body was found in the basement, wedged behind a water heater under the stairs. This was Dutoits' son, Christopher Emmanuel, three months old.

The infant had a plastic bag tied around his head and a wooden stake through his heart.

The baby's parents had also died before the fire, stabbed to death with a knife that was found near their bodies and dragged into the basement near their child.

The local police would later discover in interviews with former sect members that the baby had been ritually murdered several days earlier by cult members on the order of DiMambro, who claimed that the child was the anti-Christ described in the Book of Revelation. DiMambro reportedly was incensed that the parents had chosen to conceive the child without his permission.

The Canadian chalet where the bodies were found

had been elaborately booby-trapped, and there were indications the explosion had been set off by people who fled the scene beforehand. Explosive devices had been fashioned from electric coils and wired to bags of gasoline, set by timers to explode at five A.M.

The night before the bodies were found, Jouret and DiMambro had been seen leaving the chalet. Investigators believe they took a ten o'clock flight to Switzerland. Their plane was just about due to land in Zurich when the Canadian chalet burst into flames.

At first, police believed that the two key leaders of the sect, Jouret and DiMambro, the seventy-year-old financial genius and "enforcer" of the Temple, had perpetrated the mass suicide-murder and then fled. But dental charts showed that DiMambro's was one of those burned beyond recognition. And a few days later, so was Jouret's.

The unlikely duo—a personable young physician and a dour, retired businessman with a violent streak—had planned the events carefully. At lunchtime, after arriving from Canada, Jouret and Di Mambro had driven to the village of Salvan. It was early in the season; the skiers who had begun turning the area into a resort in recent years weren't expected to start trickling in for another month or so. Nevertheless, Jouret and DiMambro shopped like they were planning a party. Among their purchases were dozens of boxes of plastic trash bags. Claiming they had forgotten their keys, they also enlisted the aid of the town locksmith to open the doors of the sprawling mountainside chalet. The locksmith would later recall noticing the strong smell of gasoline in the chalet. After

Jouret and DiMambro opened up the houses, the cars of other followers began winding their way up the mountain to the chalet meeting place.

Swiss police believe that after that, Jouret and DiMambro made the seventy-five-minute drive to Cheiry, where the sect maintained a temple and conference center at the farmhouse, to supervise the killings, suicides, and arson there. Then they drove back to the Salvan ski area for the final phase of death, which included their own.

Again, there were indications that not everyone had gone willingly to their deaths in Salvan. In apartments that had been rented in the area by some of the victims, suitcases were found fully packed, suggesting that their owners believed they might be about to embark on a somewhat more worldly trip. Where that might have been remained a mystery.

In the village of Salvan, where they gathered often for weekend retreats, Solar Temple members had been an object of curiosity for many months among the permanent population of about a hundred. Locals found the sect's expensive cars and well-heeled tastes curious.

However, Solar Temple members kept to themselves and gave no one cause to report them to the police. In Salvan, a waitress at the village restaurant told reporters, "Dr. Jouret was tall and handsome and behaved quite normally. I never saw anything odd about him."

In Cheiry, villagers felt both shock and fear in the days after their rural calm was shattered by the flames and explosions inside the farmhouse, and from the world attention that followed.

"God speaks through events, like the phenomenon

of sects," Reverend Claude Morel told a congregation in a church near the village. Another cleric, Reverend Jean Richoz, told his flock that "sects are signs of demonic influence."

But as investigators unraveled the clues left behind, it appeared that money, not supernatural demons, had a lot to do with the horrors of December 5. At the time of the mass deaths, there were an estimated 400 to 500 members of the Solar Temple, perhaps a hundred of whom were in Canada. In recent months the group had been roiled by dissension over money, much of it centering on the freewheeling spending habits of Jouret and DiMambro.

Some followers saw disaster coming and managed to avoid it. In an interview with the French weekly *L'Express,* Patrick Vaurnet, a twenty-six-year-old former member, said that in Solar Temple meetings in the year before the disaster, "the theme of the transit from life to death came up more and more," and that Jouret had assured members that death was nothing to fear. Vaurnet is the son of Jean Vaurnet, a French businessman and former Olympic champion skier. The elder Vaurnet said he did not know that his son had been a member of the sect.

Who was Luc Jouret?

Jouret was born in 1947 in the Belgian Congo, now Zaire. Later, his brother would recall him as sociable, intelligent, and intensely competitive as a boy. As a young man, Jouret returned to his parents' country of Belgium and served in the army. After the army he studied medicine in Brussels, graduating in 1974 from the Free University of Brussels with a degree in medicine. His original intent was to specialize in obstetrics, but in time he became involved in homeopathic healing—which depends on using small amounts of chemicals and other natural substances to attempt cures for disease.

Jouret dabbled in mysticism and was fascinated with the rituals, intrigues, and trappings of secret societies, especially the fourteenth century Order of the Knights Templar, a French cult with militarist proclivities that claimed to be descended from the warrior Knights Templar of the Crusades. After the final Crusade in the thirteenth century, the historical Knights Templar dispersed throughout Europe and the Mediterranean, but maintained their ties and used the immense financial resources they had amassed to establish international secret networks of finance, influence, and political power. Their most successful financial achievement was to establish an influential international banking system that controlled the national debts of France and England for generations.

In 1307, King Philip the Fair of France confiscated Templar properties and had dozens of their leaders publicly executed. Templar leaders throughout Europe were also executed, effectively destroying the organization. However, the persecutions created a romantic and mystical legend, and from then on hundreds of sects arose around the world—many of them merely fraternal, theological or scholarly in nature, but some conspiratorial and fanatically religious—claiming to be the heirs of the Templars.

The Solar Temple was such a group. It claimed a lineage traced to the fourteenth century secret Order and later resurrected as a branch of European Freemasonry that admitted only Christians. By the 1970s, Jouret had found his way into a modern French offshoot that called itself the Renewed Order of the Temple. The Renewed Order augmented the mysticism and intrigues of the medieval Templar orders with measures of neo-Nazi occultism and Indian transcendentalism. It also adopted theatrical techniques—costumes, incantations, and rituals—straight from Hollywood horror movies. The Renewed Order had its headquarters in a medieval château in France, not far from the Belgian border. At the time Luc Jouret found his way into its membership, the Renewed Order was still led by a former Gestapo officer named Julien Origas.

Jouret was philosophically restless. In 1977, while experimenting in southwest France with organic nutrition and herbal medicine, he visited the Philippines and became intrigued with psychic healers who claimed to cure diseases and make tumors disappear. During a year spent traveling in Asia, primarily India, he reported a spiritual awakening. By the time he returned home he had decided to switch his practice to homeopathic medicine, and set up a practice in an Ardennes village. Around that time, he was married briefly, had a child who died in infancy, and was soon afterward divorced.

He steadily rose through the secret ranks of the Renewed Order, meanwhile. But in the mid-eighties, after a power clash following the death of Origas, and while quarreling over finances with other sect members, Jouret set out on his own. With a small group of followers, he moved to Switzerland and founded the International Chivalric Order Solar Tradition, called Solar Temple for short. It in turn absorbed an existing sect in Geneva led by DiMambro called Foundation Golden Way. After the merger, the organization was headed by Jouret, who functioned as its religious leader and philosopher. To the mystical base that was already in place, Jouret added a modern blend of New Age spiritualism, apocalyptic environmentalism, homeopathic medicine, and—in a nod to the decade in which the movement had its greatest growth—high finance. The financial end was the responsibility of DiMambro, a prosperous investor who handled the bank accounts and also maintained group discipline.

With Jouret acting in the role of high priest, the group in Switzerland coalesced around the idea that the apocalypse would arrive, soon, in the form of a great cosmic ecological disaster. The Solar Temple was organized to draw loyalists ever closer to the central theme of submission and paranoia. As adherents approached that center, the belief grew more intense that here alone could be found the definitions of true reality in a universe of conflicting claims. Rituals often ended with wine, champagne, and food, and animated conversation.

Ecology was theology in the Solar Temple.

"Scenarios of ecological disaster have become particularly prominent among contemporary apocalyptic sectarians, especially those influenced by New Age ideas," Michael Barkun, an authority on racist cults at Syracuse University wrote in the *Los Angeles Times* after the disaster. "At a time when many natural disasters have lost their power to shock, and the end of the Cold War has reduced fears of a nuclear holocaust, environmental disasters emerge as a potent expression that the world is ending."

Unlike Old Testament authoritarian cult charismatics such as Jim Jones and David Koresh, Luc Jouret maintained control using techniques of group coercion and management that he perfected over the years in a sideline as a free-lance corporate motivational lecturer and facilitator. But for his followers, the effect was chillingly similar. When summoned by Jouret, they dropped everything and heeded the call, and they died for it.

Over the years, Jouret energetically recruited new members—people with money to pay the steep Solar Temple "dues." Many of these first entered his influence through a homeopathic clinic Jouret ran in Geneva, where he told patients, "A physician should also be a priest."

Switzerland, with its ample farmland, liberal banking laws, central location, affluent population, and traditional tolerance toward offbeat religious movements, was an ideal location for such an organization. Switzerland has in recent years become a hotbed of millenarian religious activity, drawing believers from all over the world who are convinced the world is about to end. With its well-established reputation as a refuge from war, a haven of civility and prosperity, Switzerland had became an international center of new religions and cult activities.

Many of them are peaceable New Age and gnostic groups claiming to trace their lineage to pre-Christian and pagan sects. They seek "a safe place in Switzerland," said Massimo Introvigne, head of the Center for Studies on New Religions.

The two bases of the Solar Temple, Geneva and

Montreal, "have the richest variety of esoteric and gnostic groups in the world," Introvigne said.

Such groups claim membership of about 200,000 in Switzerland, which has an overall population of 7 million.

The Solar Temple, with its moralistic advocacy of organic farming, brandishing its politically correct cachet of the "Green" environmental movement, adroitly attracted lots of disaffiliated but nevertheless wealthy and educated followers, some of whom had been recruited to Switzerland by Jouret on his frequent travels throughout Europe and to Canada and Australia.

"His followers were not backpackers on the Katmandu trail," a Swiss historian who had been studying the Solar Temple at the time of the disaster told the *Sunday Times* of London. "One of the most surprising features about them is that they were respectable and sometimes prominent people. They led ordinary lives but had been converted to his message."

The trouble that spelled doom for Jouret started not in Switzerland, where the group was left alone, but in Canada, where Jouret had an active following but came to believe the sect was being persecuted.

Around 1986 the restless Jouret and DiMambro had led a handful of French and Swiss followers to a new settlement that they called the "Promised Land" in Quebec province, which, Jouret believed, was one of the few places on earth that would largely escape the ecological calamity he insisted was about to destroy the rest of the world. Jouret and DiMambro purchased a former monastery with 1,000 acres of farmland in a rural Laurentian area about fifty miles north of Montreal. The land was cultivated by followers who raised organic vegetables. Members, who also operated a bakery and were expected to contribute their worldly possessions to the group, lived in a commune, while Jouret and DiMambro enjoyed the luxury of the ski resort.

"We knew they were a religious commune of some sort, but they never bothered anybody," the town secretary told reporters. But town resident Jeanine Brenon gave the *Toronto Star* a different view: "They frightened me. All this dark talk of famines and fire and apocalypse . . ."

Like Roch Theriault and his Ant Hill Kids, Jouret and his followers found fertile philosophical ground in Quebec, where homeopathic healing groups flourish and the organic farming and other ecological movements have spawned literally thousands of rural New Age communities.

In Canada, Jouret was known as a skilled speaker and an ingenious social "networker" who quickly branched out from the rural environment to the corporate realm, where the money was. He moved skillfully into the burgeoning corporate motivational business—where inspirational lecturers and so-called facilitators sponsor improvement and self-realization seminars that many businesses require employees to attend.

Jouret was especially successful with Hydro-Quebec, the big regional power company. In 1988 and 1989 he was hired by Hydro-Quebec to present a series of motivational seminars to employees, with topics such as "Self-Realization and Management." In these seminars, Jouret gradually identified likely recruits, and then spent extra effort to lure them from the philosophical periphery of business dynamics and office relationships toward the darker circles of authoritarianism, paranoia, and ultimate submission. It was a measure of his success at just one company that after the holocaust in Switzerland, Hydro-Quebec officials said that seventeen of its employees still had links to the Solar Temple.

At the same time, Jouret kept busy traveling to small cities and towns to recruit followers with lectures on homeopathic medicine and organic nutrition. Authorities believed that Jouret attracted several hundred followers in Quebec to add to the estimated three hundred Solar Temple members in Switzerland and France. Throughout the years he spent in Canada, Jouret and DiMambro traveled frequently to Switzerland, to maintain their hold over followers there and to supervise new recruiting efforts.

By 1993, Jouret's cultlike organization had achieved a deft fusion of the 1980s and the 1990s, blending aggressive financial energy with New Age narcissism. Holding it all together was the usual specter of authoritarianism in which petty rules about food and behavior were rigidly enforced.

The Solar Temple had three distinct membership tiers. The lowest level cost about fifty dollars a week in dues and was largely comprised of new recruits who attended lectures and bought motivational tapes. The next level was called Club Arcadia and cost about $150 a week. Its members became more closely involved in Solar Temple religious rituals and recruiting activities, and worked in the cult's organic farming businesses. The highest rank, which cost about $200 a week in dues, was called the Golden Circle, and its members were designated the chevalier order and conducted secret rituals, magical and occult in tone. The chevaliers formed the inner circle around Jouret and DiMambro.

Besides paying dues through day jobs or other sources, members of the two top levels were expected to donate property and savings to the Solar Temple.

But Solar Temple hierarchy does not seem to have indulged itself in the perverted or promiscuous activity that characterizes the leadership of other killer cults, although some complained that Jouret maintained the right to approve marriages and to dissolve them at will. Instead, focus was intensely centered on organization and cohesion, with the internal creative strain to ensure discipline in the belief that only a hundred of the group would form the Elected, those who would be transported from this world en masse to survive the end of time.

The public heard little about Jouret's activities in Canada until 1993, when police placed the Solar Temple under surveillance on suspicion of weapons violations. Later that year, Jouret pleaded guilty to a weapons charge in Canada. He was fined $750 for the charge, which involved the possession of illegal gun silencers.

In the publicity surrounding that case, Rose-Marie Klaus, one of the Solar Temple members who had followed Jouret and DiMambro to Canada from

Switzerland, told a Radio Canada reporter that she
and her husband had given Jouret and DiMambro
$500,000 to invest in the organic farm before leaving
the sect in disgust. "Jouret told people that a great
cataclysm is going to take place and that only the
elected will survive. He persuaded several people to
leave Europe, sell everything, and invest in his proj-
ects. Jouret thinks he's Christ."

Canadian police later theorized that Jouret and
DiMambro began discussing the mass suicide and
killing in March 1993, during the investigation into
the weapons allegations, when police raided a burial
crypt the Order maintained near Morin Heights.
That raid evidently prompted Jouret and DiMambro
to abandon their dream of setting up a Promised
Land in Canada.

Furious about the publicity that Klaus and other
critics had managed to attract after the weapons
plea, Jouret apparently left Canada in disgust in late
1993 and returned only sporadically during the last
year of his life.

But the trouble in Canada followed him back to
Switzerland. Among those dead in the Swiss chalets
were Canadian followers who had told friends they
were flying to Switzerland to confront Jouret over
the sect's financial affairs. These Canadians included
sect members Robert Ostiguy, fifty years old, a businessman and mayor of Richelieu, a small city about
twenty-five miles south of Montreal; Joce-Lyne
Grand'Maison, forty-four, a reporter for the newspaper *Le Journal de Quebec;* and Robert Falardeau,
forty-seven, a minor official of the Quebec finance
ministry who had abandoned his job and flown to

Switzerland several months earlier to help straighten out "questionable" business dealings in the group.

According to a Montreal newspaper, Ostiguy had secretly joined the sect in the late 1980s. The other two also kept their membership secret. There were other reports that Jouret had recently been replaced as Grand Master of the Canadian branch of the Temple, deepening the rifts.

Some of the dissension may have been merely strategic. As real estate portfolios lost value during the 1990s, assets declined in value and Solar Temple investment income dropped sharply. Some current and former members who survived spoke of growing tensions because of the vast sums of money invested by DiMambro and Jouret in property. Others remarked that in Canada there was growing dissent over Jouret's arbitrariness in approving and sometimes capriciously dissolving marriages between members.

Jouret always kept up his frantic traveling pace. For years he had remained active in Australia, where he and DiMambro visited frequently in the second half of the eighties, networking among New Age groups there. Jouret had plans to hold regular religious services at Ayers Rock, a huge formation that rises in the desert of Uluru-Kata Tjuta National Park, and which has become a kind of religious shrine for New Age spiritualists. However, the local aborigine community, which controls access to the site, refused him permission. Nevertheless, Jouret continued his travels and organizing in Australia.

*   *   *

The trigger to the tragedy of October 5, 1994, evidently, was money. After the deaths, investigators in Canada quickly discovered millions of dollars of deposits by DiMambro and Jouret in the banks on three continents. DiMambro, who had spend six months in a Canadian jail on a fraud conviction in 1972, was found to have owned more than sixty properties. His personal credit-card charges were averaging about $35,000 a month at the time of his death.

There also were reports that the Canadian police had been investigating DiMambro for illegally laundering as much of $95 million. A few days after the bodies were discovered in Canada and Switzerland, Royal Canadian Mounted Police Constable Gilles Deziel confirmed to reporters in Montreal that the federal police agency had "an ongoing investigation of money-laundering involving certain members of the Order of the Solar Temple." But he declined to identify those being investigated.

There were also reports that police suspected Jouret had been linked to a right-wing paramilitary group called Q-37 and had plotted to blow up Hydro-Quebec transmission towers and made threats against government officials.

At the same time, Canadian police for several years had been looking into reports that Jouret and his followers there were stockpiling weapons and plotting to infiltrate government and business organizations.

A few days after the deaths, the French interior ministry received a letter from the Solar Temple—mailed in Geneva the day of the tragedy—that denounced the "relentlessness" of government investigations of the cult.

"Faced with the police intimidation that we are constantly victims of . . . we have decided, in all consciousness, to leave this world," the letter said, according to the *Toronto Star.*

Jouret and DiMambro had spent much of 1994 shuttling back and forth between Switzerland and Canada. In Quebec during the latter part of the year, Jouret began warning followers that the "Day of Cataclysm" was at head. He meant it.

Police later were told that cult members were convinced that they would be reborn on a distant planet they called Sirius after passing through a fiery death on earth.

Robert Falardeau, the minor finance ministry official who was believed to have been the leader of the Canadian branch of the cult, apparently returned to Canada from Switzerland late in September 1994. During the last week of the month, he stayed at Hotel Bonivard in Veytauxa. Hotel employees said that on the night of September 26, Falardeau received a mysterious phone call and left hurriedly, indicating there was an emergency. Police believe Farardeau urgently flew to Switzerland that night or the next morning.

A few nights after that, Jouret was seen with DiMambro attending a tense dinner with seven others in a private dining room of the hotel. Umberto Timmoneri, supervisor of the restaurant, told the *Toronto Star,* "They were tense and had a serious air about them. Visibly, they had very low morale. I shudder to think that it may have been here that they finalized their disastrous massacre."

And two nights before the killings, DiMambro and twelve close followers in Canada had a ritualistic "Last Supper" at an expensive restaurant nearby. Jouret did not attend.

Looking at it strictly as a criminal case, money was the most immediate cause of the disaster. There was so much at stake. As authorities began to unravel the secrets, they turned up a huge bank account in Austria, where banking sources described for a Swiss newspaper how a DiMambro associate opened up an account there in 1993 with a fortune—some sources placed the amount at more than $90 million—in money transferred from a Swiss bank. According to police, Jouret and DiMambro spent most of the winter of 1994 in the Australian state of Queensland.

But money does not explain why so many cult members in Switzerland went willingly to their deaths. The money problems were largely hidden from the followers in Switzerland and France, who came when Jouret called them because they believed in the literal truth that doomsday was on its way and that the Solar Temple provided the means to achieve "purification" through the cosmic fire and to rise from the ashes of destructive humankind as higher evolutionary life forms.

Some experts claimed that New Age cults—driven by modern marketing techniques, keyed to environmental moralism—are spreading more rapidly than the older millenarian cults based on Protestant Christianity and a literal interpretation of the Book of Revelation. While most New Age cults are much more likely to focus on spiritualism and self-improvement, the Solar Temple was a quick reminder that killer cults can take on new forms and blaze with the same degree of extremism that brought the multitudes to die in Jonestown and Waco.

Professor Peter Bayer of the University of Toronto's religious studies department told the *Toronto Star,* "The religious marketplace is wide open to an entrepreneur to create a unique product."

Always a marketing genius, Luc Jouret's deadly new religious product was carefully designed for New Age appeal. Former followers recalled visits to Stonehenge, and midnight ceremonies beneath a full moon where druidlike priests in hooded robes embroidered with crosses chanted slogans, and Jouret urged them all to prepare for the apocalypse.

A sixty-three-year-old villager in Cheiry on that night recalled the awe and confusion:

"There was a little fire, then a big flame, then the gas canisters went off. I first thought they were having a party, with firecrackers. Then it really started burning."

Hours later he learned what had happened.

"It was horrible," he said, "a temple of death."